G000130909

PRENTICE HALL

Language Teaching Methodology Series

Classroom Techniques and Resources

General Editor: Christopher N. Candlin

Songs in Action

Salesian English Language Centre

SALESIAN COLLEGE,
CELBRIDGE,
CO. KILDARE,
IRELAND.

Other titles in this series include:

ARGONDIZZO, Carmen
Children in action

DORNYEI, Zoltan and THURRELL, Sarah
Conversation and dialogues in action

FRANK, Christine and RINVOLUCRI, Mario
Grammar in action again

GERNGROSS, Gunter and PUCHTA, Herbert
Pictures in action

GOLEBIOWSKA, Aleksandra
Getting students to talk

McKAY, Sandra
Teaching grammar

NUNAN, David
Language teaching methodology

NUNAN, David
Understanding language classrooms

PECK, Antony
Language teachers at work

ROST, Michael
Listening in action

STEMPLESKI, Susan and TOMALIN, Barry
Video in action

STEVICK, Earl
Success with foreign languages

TAYLOR, Linda
Vocabulary in action

TAYLOR, Linda
Teaching and learning vocabulary

WINGATE, Jim
Getting beginners to talk

YALDEN, Janice
The communicative syllabus

Songs in Action

DALE T. GRIFFEE
Seigakuin University, Japan

ENGLISH LANGUAGE TEACHING

Prentice Hall
New York   London   Toronto   Sydney   Tokyo   Singapore

First published 1992 by
Prentice Hall International (UK) Ltd
66 Wood Lane End, Hemel Hempstead
Hertfordshire HP2 4RG
A division of
Simon & Schuster International Group

© Prentice Hall International (UK) Ltd, 1992

All rights reserved. No part of this publication may be
reproduced, stored in a retrieval system, or transmitted,
in any form, or by any means, electronic, mechanical,
photocopying, recording or otherwise, without prior
permission, in writing, from the publisher.
For permission within the United States of America
contact Prentice Hall Inc., Englewood Cliffs, NJ 07632.

Typeset in 10½/12½pt Times
by MHL Typesetting Ltd, Coventry

Printed and bound in Great Britain by
Dotesios Ltd, Trowbridge, Wiltshire.

Library of Congress Cataloging-in-Publication Data

Griffee, Dale.
    Songs in action / Dale T. Griffee.
        p.   cm. — (English language teaching) (Language teaching
    methodology series)
    Includes bibliographical references (p.   ) and indexes.
    ISBN 0-13-824988-1
        1. English language—Study and teaching—Foreign speakers.
    2. Music in education. I. Title. II. Series. III. Series:
    Language teaching methodology series.
    PE1128.A2G69   1992
    428'.007—dc20   91-30436
                                                              CIP

British Library Cataloguing in Publication Data

Griffee, Dale, T.
    Songs in Action. — (Language teaching
    methodology series)
    I. Title II. Series
    428

ISBN 0-13-950916-X

1 2 3 4 5   96 95 94 93 92

To Norma Vinnedge who sang me my first song,
Arnold Bourziel who introduced me to music,
George Flora who gave the experience of music and
Joseph Wesley Mathews who revealed to me the mystery of music.

Contents

Preface

With the Language Teaching Methodology Series we have created a special set of books with the *In Action* title. These books are designed to offer teachers material that can be directly used in class. They are resources for action, hence the title. They offer language teachers material which can be adapted with various inputs for their own classroom work. The activities are presented in an accessible and teacher-friendly way, with a clear identification of teacher and learner roles, and above all, they consist of tried and tested tasks. The authors of the books in the *In Action* collection all have considerable practical experience of teaching and of classroom research. It is this combination of principle and practice, available in an easily accessible form for the teacher, which characterises the design of the books. We hope that they will not only help teachers to plan and carry out exciting lessons but also to develop themselves as reflective teachers by suggesting action research that can be done with their own learners.

Songs in Action is not just a collection of activities to provide light relief for learners (and for teachers) at the end of a long and tiring week. To be sure, songs have a place in the classroom for helping create that friendly and co-operative atmosphere so important for language learning, but they can offer much more. They offer insights into the culture and especially the stories and myths of different societies, providing a window into the frames of reference and values of the peoples whose language we are learning. They offer a rich background and a social and historical context to language learning. More than that, however, they are themselves vehicles for language, offering to the learner opportunities for practice of otherwise often difficult areas of intonation and rhythm as well as ways into particular vocabulary fields. They thus provide both language learning content and language learning process, both subject-matter to be learned as well as practice in language learning. All teachers know how popular the lyrics and music of English songs are for a wide range of learners. They know how much out-of-classroom time is devoted to their extra-curricular practice! With this new contribution from Dale Griffee to the *In Action* series, teachers can turn this student energy to good effect and locate it inside the classroom, not only outside. As with the other books in the collection, Dale Griffee has organised the activities according to useful categories of language learning skill, language topic, types of learner and types of classroom activity. He has provided a very valuable bibliography for teachers to follow up their interests and has suggested a variety of lesson plans in which songs are integrated in a variety of different ways. In addition, and in keeping with the objectives of the collection, he has suggested a range of action research tasks that teachers can undertake in their classes, using songs as a trigger for learning. Above all, the book stays close to the learner, making use of his or her own delight and interest in songs and singing and showing how language learning can be truly a lyrical experience!

As General Editor, I hope that the books in this new *In Action* collection will continue the success of the Language Teaching Methodology Series more generally in developing the skills and knowledge of the reflective language teacher in the classroom.

Professor Christopher N. Candlin
General Editor

Acknowledgements

Writing a book is a personal journey, but one can get lost without guides and friends. I would like to thank those who have helped me along the way. First, I would like to thank David Haines for inviting me to contribute this volume to the Prentice Hall Language Teaching Methodology Series and Christopher Candlin, series editor, for providing suggestions and guidance.

I owe thanks to Fraida Dubin, Roy Kingsbury, Virginia LoCastro, Tim Murphy, Jack Richards and Nina Weinstein. I am also indebted to Norma Simmons for research assistance and to Shirley L. Capron of the Donald B. Watt Library, School for International Training, Brattleboro, Vermont for her never-failing support. Also to Julian Bamford, Marc Helgesen and Joanne Sauber for advice and suggestions which they gave freely; to Doreen Blas, Steve Brown, Karl Diller, Greta Gorsuch, Shaun McNally, Dorolyn Smith and Catherine Tansey for reading and commenting on various drafts; to David P. Benseler of the *Modern Language Journal* for his encouragement and help over a period of years; and especially to Claire Stanley of the MAT programme, School for International Training.

I am indebted to numerous teachers and writers, some directly and some indirectly, for many of the song and music ideas, techniques and extensions collected in this book: Keiko Abe, Jayne Halsne Abrate, Barry Baddock, Kathi Bailey, Julian Bamford, G. Bartle, Moshi Barzilai, Marilyn Books, James W. Brown, Steve Brown, Don Campbell, Peter Carney, Gillian Dickinson, Patricia Dissoway, Jayne Gaunt, Manual Gelman, James Gordon, Marc Helgesen, Ursula Holzer, Mitsuko Hosoya, Shawn Keys, Roy Kingsbury, Steve Lander, William D. Leith, Helen Loew, Alan Maley, Patricia Mathews, Don Maybin, Gertrude Moskowitz, John Morgan, Sandra Moulding, Ian Muir-Cochrane, Olivia Munoz, Tim Murphy, Patrick O'Shea, Branko Ostojic, Sandra L. Parker, Regina G. Richards, Mario Rinvolucri, Joachim Sandvoss, Joanne Sauber, R. Murray Shafer, Miho Steinberg, Julia Ann Summers, Michael Swan, Mary Techmeier, Shirley Tsai, Penny Ur, Zubeda Vahed, Jill Van Cleve, Marianne Vaney, Carl Wakamoto, Catherine Walter, Kaye Wilson, Ken Wilson, Meguido Zola.

Finally, I would like to thank my students at the University of Pittsburgh English Language Institute in Tokyo; Tokai Junior College; Fuji Electric Company, the Shinryo Corporation, the Nisho Iwai Trading Company and Wacker Chemicals East Asia Ltd, all of Tokyo; the University of New Hampshire summer English programme and finally James English School, Sendai, Japan, where this project was born. Without their participation and feedback this book would have been impossible.

Dale T. Griffee

INTRODUCTION

Introduction

Songs in Action is a book of classroom-originated and tested song activities. They were researched and tested by teachers of many languages and for that reason can be used in the teaching of any language. These song activities come from many sources: FL (foreign language) teachers, ESL (English as a second language) teachers and EFL (English as a foreign language). Consequently many of the activities are a synthesis from many sources and have many extensions, hints and suggestions for further use.

The main purpose of these activities is to give language teachers ways of working with popular-song lyrics in terms of:

1. Vocabulary

2. Listening

3. Singing

4. Writing

5. Discussion

There are also activities for working with instrumental music, activities for working with sounds and sound environments, and activities for music discussions which rely on memories and do not require any listening at all.

Throughout *Songs in Action* you will see the terms *songs* and *music*. The word *songs* refers to pieces of music that have words, especially popular songs such as those one hears on the radio. By *music* is meant instrumental music, for example, symphonic, chamber, easy listening, or solo instruments such as the organ, flute or guitar. Most of the activities are for pop songs, but many activities are for instrumental music and you can find these by looking at the Index of activities on page 169.

What makes a song a song?

Although songs have elements in common with speech and poetry, they are a unique form. Both songs and speech are vocally produced, are linguistically meaningful and have melody. Both songs and poetry use words to convey meaning, both are usually written down before publication, both can be put to music and both can be listened to (e.g. a poetry reading for poems and a concert for songs).

Nevertheless, songs have their own identity and they function differently from speech or poetry. It is possible to note at least three features of songs:

1. Songs convey a lower amount of information than poetry. Even though poetry can be heard, we usually read it, which permits longer and more dense information.

2. Songs have more redundancy than poetry. Songs achieve redundancy by devices such as the borrowing of lines from other songs, proverbs, catchphrases and cliché

as well as alliteration. It is this high degree of redundancy that makes songs sound so simple, especially when compared to the complexity and subtlety of poetry. The simplicity of songs is not, however, a weak point. Because a song is heard for a short time, simplicity, redundancy and a certain 'expectedness' contribute to our understanding.

3.   Songs have a personal quality that makes the listener react as if the song were being sung for the listener personally. We are joined through the direct quality of the song words (unlike a movie actor in a film, talking to another actor) to the singer and through the singer to others in the audience even if we are at home rather than at a concert. Thus songs have a socially unifying feature for the selected audience. Songs create their own world of feeling and emotion, and as we participate in the song, we participate in the world it creates. As Mark Booth states, 'The song embodies myth and we step into it.'

Why use popular songs?

No one knows exactly why songs are powerful, but everyone knows from a personal point of view that they are. They are non-threatening; we usually choose which songs we listen to. Songs speak to us directly about our experiences, they reassure us in our moments of trouble. They are a satisfying art form: the lyrics fit the music and the music fits the lyrics and together they form a complete unit. Another reason might be the ability of songs and music in general to affect our emotions. Many people can be moved to tears or other strong emotions by music, and songs can acquire strong emotional associations with people, events and places.

For all these reasons, there are many advantages to using songs and music in the language classroom. All of these reasons have been suggested, but the answer remains a mystery. Several reasons are listed below, in six categories: classroom atmosphere, language input, cultural input, text, supplements, teaching and student interest.

Classroom atmosphere

Songs and music can be used to relax students and provide an enjoyable classroom atmosphere. For many, learning a new language is inherently an insecure proposition. Language, our basis of communication, is taken away from us and we often feel lost and dependent. Songs, but more especially instrumental music, give us the external cover we need to feel more secure while at the same time providing the internal support to carry on with the task.

Language input

There seems to be a deep relationship between rhythm and speech. Sensitivity to rhythm is a basic and necessary first step in learning a language. In using songs and music in the classroom we are exposing students to the rhythms of language. Additionally, popular songs contain examples of colloquial speech. For example, in many songs the '-ing' form is usually reduced from the full '-ing' to just an 'n' sound, but this reduction is a regular feature of standard English. The natural language of songs, as opposed to the artificial language in many textbooks, is one way to incorporate modern, living language into the classroom.

Cultural input

Music is not universal. Music is a reflection of the time and place that produced it. Every song is a culture capsule containing within itself a significant piece of social information. Why do the songs of the 1940s sound the way they do and have the themes they do? Because they reflect not only the available sound technology of their time, but also the fears and hopes of their time. That is true for the songs of every decade. Bringing a song into the classroom entails bringing the culture of the song in with it. Additionally, songs can be used as a way of looking at a culture and comparing it with other cultures. Songs can also be used to evoke historical periods. For example, certain Christmas carols from Europe reveal the history as well as the geography of that area. Many songs are about cities and can be used to study the important sights, sounds and feelings of a city.

Song as text

Songs can be used as texts in the same way that a poem, short story or novel or any other piece of authentic material can be used. This is especially true if you, the teacher, want to develop a special course for which no text exists.

Songs and music as supplements

Songs can be used to supplement a textbook or can serve as the text itself in a variety of teaching situations such as:

1. Using a song after the regular lesson.
2. Using a song for a change of pace.
3. Using a song for special occasions such as Christmas or when the textbook has no unit on a subject.

Teaching conversation

Songs and music can be used as a launching pad for conversation in the same way that poetry or other forms of written discourse can be used: their form can be discussed or their content can offer a springboard for class discussion.

Teaching vocabulary

Songs are especially good at introducing vocabulary because songs provide a meaningful context for the vocabulary.

Teaching or reviewing grammatical structures

Songs provide a natural context for the most common structures such as verb tenses and prepositions.

Teaching pronunciation

Songs and music, with their tones, rhythm and stress, can provide for some languages a suitable way to teach and practise the several skills we group together under the term pronunciation.

Teaching and memory

Songs can be used for pattern practice and memory retention. If appropriate tasks are given, songs give pleasurable repetition with no boredom and provide active participation in the language.

Student interest

From the time of puberty to the end of our twenties, popular songs have a powerful impact on us. No one has to force us to listen to songs and music and our students are no different. They listen because they want to and we as teachers have built-in interest — ours and theirs. We can learn about the music of our students as well as teach them about our music.

Our young students are the new generation. They were born at a time in which most of them, no matter where they were born, know each other's songs, and English-language songs lead this movement. Songs are part of what makes a generation a generation and the current generation is a global generation rather than a parochial one. The world is evolving a common culture and pop songs are its backbone. By using pop songs in your classroom, you and your students are participating in the emerging world culture.

What songs should I use?

There are no rules for selecting a song for classroom use, but there are several things to take into consideration. They are listed below under four categories: the class, the teacher, classroom opportunities and the music.

The class

1. How many students and their age.
2. The time of day.
3. The language level of the students.
4. Their musical interests.

You as teacher should consider the age and interests of your class. Does your class have six students or sixteen or sixty? What is the age of the students? Are they six years old or sixteen or sixty? Consider also the time of day. Some classes in the evening are tired and need music that invigorates them, while other classes might need to have their energy level controlled a bit more. What is the language level of your class and what are their musical interests? Each age group has its own musical likes and dislikes.

The teacher

  5. Teacher's age and musical interests.
  6. What classroom support do you have?
  7. What is your purpose in using this song?

Consider any song or instrumental music selection in relation to yourself. If you are just out of school and teaching in your own country, perhaps your musical taste is not much different from that of your students. If you are more experienced or teaching in a culture not your own, your musical interests and your students' musical interests may not have much in common. It is not wise to use music that you do not like. It is also unwise to use music students do not like. The answer is to find common ground. One solution is to ask students to bring in songs they like, with the lyrics. There is a quantity of music that you and your students can both appreciate.

Classroom opportunities

  8. Do you have a high level of independence?
  9. Do you have some free class time?
10. Can you supplement a lesson?

Many chances exist for using songs and music in a classroom. One occasion is when you have a high level of freedom to determine the curriculum. This is frequently the case in private language conversation schools, some universities, school clubs and private lessons. You can use songs and music when the curriculum has been predetermined, but there is time remaining in the class period. You can use songs and music for special holidays or for weather, for example a special song and a lesson plan for rainy days. The best situation is when the song you select is a direct complement to your lesson. The song contains a structure, vocabulary or a discussion theme that can be used directly in a text lesson.

The music

11. Will the music disturb other classes?
12. Do you have a music library?
13. Does the song lesson require support and do you have it?
14. What is your lesson plan?

How will the music sound in your classroom? Some rooms are large and almost eat up sound. On the other hand, music can be played at such a volume that it disturbs other classes. What songs do you have access to? Does your school have a music library? Most teachers use songs from their own collection. Of course, it is possible to borrow songs from other sources, including your students. It is obvious that you cannot use a song you do not have in the sense of having a tape or CD. Some techniques require support such as a board and the use of a copy machine, while others can be done with no special support or preparation. Last, consider your lesson plan or what you want to accomplish with the song.

A good song to use in your classroom is a song which:

1. your students like,
2. you like,
3. fits your lesson,
4. and one which you have a copy of.

How can I get the lyrics to songs?

There are at least two good reasons for having the exact and complete lyrics to any song you use. First, if you know 99 per cent of the lyrics, but do not know one word or phrase, that is exactly the word or phrase your students will ask you about. The second reason is less pedagogical and more social. Many songs have lyrics that are socially questionable. This is especially true of certain types of rock songs. If you come across this type of lyrics, you have options: you may explain them, ignore them, decide not to use the song. You cannot exercise any of the options, however, if you are unaware of the problem. Following are some ways to acquire song lyrics.

1. Buy records, tapes or CDs that have the lyrics printed inside. In the case of tape cassettes, these printed lyrics are very small, but they can be put on a copy machine and enlarged. In many cases these lyrics contain mistakes, so be sure to check them carefully.

2. Listen to the song and write the words yourself. There are many songs that are slow enough for you to do this and many singers who sing quite clearly.

3. Ask your friends to help you when you cannot catch a certain line or phrase. While it might be asking too much of your friends to transcribe the lyrics to a complete song, most people will help you with a difficult line. Write out the lyrics and put blank spaces where you cannot catch the words. Ask your friends to listen and tell you the parts you cannot catch.

4. Use songs found in books of song lyrics. There is, for example, a paperback book that can be purchased of all the Beatles' song lyrics, and books of music with words.

5. For the latest hit songs, there are various magazines which feature song lyrics. These magazines specialise in the latest rock, punk, etc. types of music.

6. Buy ESL song collections that have a songbook with lyrics, such as the BBC *Songs Alive*, which features ten traditional English songs. All the songs in this collection are songs that tell stories and the BBC has a video tape in addition to a very good audio tape. See pages 160–2 for a listing of ESL songbooks.

7. Get together with other teachers and share your work. Listen and transcribe a song, make a copy and pass it around while another colleague does the same. Gradually you can acquire a fairly good collection. You might be able to contact teachers at other schools or co-ordinate your efforts through a professional teaching association such as JALT (the Japan Association of Language Teachers), TESOL (Teachers of English to Speakers of Other Languages) or IATEFL (International Association of Teachers of English as a Foreign Language).

8. Assign students the job of writing the lyrics. This can be done either in class or for homework. You can help them by listening to the song and reviewing their work.

How can I use *Songs in Action*?

There are several ways you can use this book. One is to turn immediately to the song activities on page 169 and read through the activities until you find one or more that catch your eye. Each activity is designed to be used independently, but some activities complement each other while others are mutually exclusive. Most activities include suggestions for follow-up.

The skill index on pages 170–1 and the level index on page 172 enable you to select activities according to the needs of your class. By experimenting, you can devise your own lesson plans.

Another way to use this book is to turn to the Appendix: Sample lesson plans and selected songs on pages 163–6. There you will find a discussion of many of the issues facing language teachers such as:

1. How many activities are appropriate for one song?
2. What are some workable combinations of activities?
3. What are some examples of the different types of songs mentioned in the activities?

You will also find different types of songs described and activities that work well with that particular type of song. These lesson plans are not a substitute for your own experimentation and the suggested activities that accompany each song type are not the only ones that could be used. Their only purpose is to get you started.

The activities in this book are grouped into five sections:

1. Vocabulary Extension.
2. Listening Development.
3. Singing Development.
4. Writing Development.
5. Discussion.

Each activity is numbered consecutively. See page 169 for a complete listing of activities. Following the number and title of the activity is the secondary focus. In the example below, the activity is mainly listening, but it also deals with writing, discussion and grammatical structures. Also applying to each activity are four indicators. The first is song type. This shows the type of song with which the activity is most compatible, although there may be exceptions. The example, 35 Lists, can be used with all types of songs: short and slow songs, short and fast songs, songs that tell stories and long, fast songs. For a more complete discussion of song types see pages 11–12. Next is level. Level matches the activity to a range of student levels. For example, 35 Lists is appropriate for students who range from very low to intermediate. Third is purpose, which summarises the activity at a glance. Finally, although all the activities can be used with adults (post-secondary school) the student indicator shows which activities could be appropriate for children as well.

35 Lists

Secondary focus: writing
discussion
grammar

Song type: all songs

Level: very low to intermediate

Purpose: classifying vocabulary

Students: adults and children

Each activity begins with an introductory paragraph or sentence which gives a quick overview.

Preparation   gives teacher preparation for the activity.

In class   gives step-by-step directions. Extensions, variations, hints and options are included if applicable.

Links   give related activities.

What are song types?

Songs are usually classified according to popularity (Top 40) or according to certain established musical forms (pop, country, folk, jazz, etc.). These classification schemes are not appropriate for language teachers because they overlook the role of the activities language teachers use. *Songs in Action* introduces a new way of classifying songs. Songs will be divided according to length and tempo, because length and tempo have a high degree of relevance to the appropriateness of a song and an activity.

1. 'All songs' means that the activity can be used with any song.

2. 'Short, slow songs' means the activity works best with songs that are slow and short. Most songs range from three and a half to four and a half minutes in length. A short song is any song that is three minutes or less.

    A typical short, slow song is *White Christmas*. For a sample listing of short and slow songs see 'A selection of short and slow songs' in Appendix: Sample lesson plans and selected songs, pages 164—5.

3. 'Songs that tell stories' are songs that have a story line. Songs that tell stories have a beginning, a middle and an end. They are usually long and slow although a very few are short and slow or short and fast. A typical example is the song *Waltzing Matilda* or *A Boy Named Sue*. For a sample listing of songs that tell stories see 'A selection of songs that tell stories' in Appendix: Sample lesson plans and selected songs, p. 165.

4. 'Instrumental music' is any music without words. For example, classical, popular instrumental or New Age music.

5. 'Long songs' are the majority of songs on Top 40 charts. They are usually at least four minutes long or longer, they are usually not very easy to sing and present a series of images rather than tell a story. Most of them are fast, although a few are slow. For many of our students, this type of song is synonymous with rock music.

6. 'Short, fast songs' are songs that typically have one verse with no repeating phrases or refrains and have a quick tempo. They are usually under three minutes in

duration. Two examples are *My Favourite Things* from *The Sound of Music* and *I'm on Fire* by Bruce Springsteen.

A final word

A collection such as this is never complete. If you do not find your favourite song or music activity, or if you know of an activity not in this book, I would be grateful if you would bring it to my attention, care of the publisher.

SECTION 1

VOCABULARY EXTENSION

Introduction

This section includes activities whose primary aim is to concentrate on the vocabulary in the song. These activities are designed to give teachers ways to explain and enrich student vocabulary. It is characteristic of modern pop songs that they use common phrases, slang, catchphrases and language from non-standard dialects. It is also characteristic of songs that they use poetic or even idiosyncratic language. These tendencies often involve low-frequency vocabulary which will need some explaining.

1 Vocabulary prediction

**Secondary
focus:**   listening

Song type: all songs

Level: very low to intermediate

Purpose: to predict vocabulary

Students: adults and children

This activity makes use of the fact that many songs have a clearly stated theme and vocabulary directly related to that theme. Students are given the theme of the song and asked to guess or predict what vocabulary they expect to hear.

Preparation

No special preparation is needed.

In class

Tell students the theme of the song. You might give them the title and background of the song. Ask them to predict words they might hear. Write the words on the board, then ask students to listen to the song and check the words they heard.

Your board might look like this

Theme, title or background information written here.					
Words	that	students	expect	or	guess
that	they	might	hear	can	be
written	on	the	board	and	then
copied	by	the	class.		

16

Extension

List a group of words which includes vocabulary from the song as well as some distracters. Listen to the song and ask students to circle the words they heard.

Links

See **Did you hear it? (30).** For a similar activity see **Vocabulary association (9).** For sample lesson plans see Appendix, page 163.

2 Drawing the song

Secondary focus: listening
grammar (prepositions)
discussion

Song type: all songs

Level: very low to intermediate

Purpose: to interpret the song visually

Students: adults and children

Visual images clarify definitions and make remembering vocabulary words easier. There are several possibilities:

1. Draw objects and places mentioned in the song. Write the name of the item under each drawing. This example is from the song *I Left My Heart in San Francisco*. Continue with **The cloze passage (23).** Cloze out the words you drew pictures of.

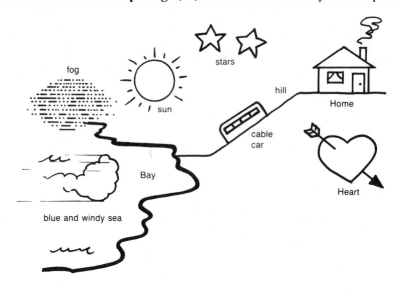

2. For a higher-level class or as a review, listen to the song and ask students to draw a scene from the song or a scene they feel appropriate and then discuss the pictures.

3. Dictate the drawing to the students. Practise prepositions of locations such as above, over, next to, slightly to the left, etc. For example, draw a hill and at the top of the hill draw a house and under the house write the word home.

4. Ask students to draw their personal responses to a song or an instrumental music selection. For example, listen to a song such as *The Marvellous Toy* and ask students to draw a favourite toy they had as a child.

Links

See **Pictures (3)** for a way to use magazine pictures or calendar art that illustrates the vocabulary. See **Song posters (48)** for suggestions on putting drawings on the wall or bulletin board.

3 Pictures

Secondary focus: listening
discussion

Song type: all songs

Level: very low to intermediate

Purpose: to interpret the song visually

Students: adults and children

Pictures from magazines, travel brochures or calendars help students remember vocabulary and create a stronger image of the song.

Preparation

Make a list of all the vocabulary in the song that could be illustrated by a picture of some sort, e.g. colour words, objects, locations and names of cities. Decide if you want to list the vocabulary on the board. Gather the pictures.

In class

Show the pictures to the class to identify the vocabulary items. Discuss.

Extensions

1. Show the pictures and ask the class to guess the type of song, e.g. love, country, rock etc. or which vocabulary items might be in the song.

2. Show the class the pictures after they have listened, instead of before, and discuss.

3. Select a picture with a theme that is related to the song and ask students for their personal reaction. For a song about city life, show a picture of a city and ask a question such as what city they would like to visit, or a city they remember as a child, or what is the best city to live in today?

Links

For additional activities that use pictures and images see **Jumbled words (22), Scrambled lyrics (37), Song corner (38), Song posters (48)** and **Picture selection (55).**

4 Rods to tell the story

Secondary focus:	listening
Song type:	songs that tell stories
Level:	low to intermediate
Purpose:	to interpret the song visually
Students:	adults and children

Algebricks or Cuisenaire Rods are wooden or plastic sticks of various lengths and colours. They can be used to help students to visualise a song that has a story or that has a clearly stated situation.

Preparation

You will need a box of rods. Coloured pencils or strips of paper can also be used but pencils tend to roll around and not stay where you put them and paper is not sturdy. Select a rod for each character in the song. Decide which other objects or locations mentioned in the song you want to depict.

In class

Tell the story in the song using the rods. Students can practise telling the story to each other.

Hint

This is a deceptively simple technique. If you are doing this for the first time, practise telling the story to a colleague or even to yourself if no one is available.

Links

For related techniques see **Tell them a story (17), Mini musicals (40)** or **Guided story writing (46).**

5   Rhyme after rhyme

Secondary focus: listening
discussion

Song type: short songs

Level: low to intermediate

Purpose: to predict rhymes

Students: adults

This activity practises rhyme and gives students a chance to make up rhymes of their own.

Preparation

Pick a song that has a clear rhyme scheme.

In class

Give the students every other line and ask them to fill in the missing lines. Ask students to read their new lyrics. Finally, listen to the original lyrics to compare.

Hint

For lower-level students or students not familiar with the concept of rhyme, underline the first word in a pair of rhyme words and cloze the second. For example:

Sleighbells ring, are you *listening*?
In the lane, snow is _____.

Links

For related techniques see **Song poetry (15), Headlines (19)** and **Abstract words (69).**

6   Scrambled words

Secondary focus: discussion

Song type: all songs

Level: low to intermediate

Purpose: preteach vocabulary

Students: adults

This is a vocabulary exercise that preteaches song vocabulary by asking students to divide into groups and look at a vocabulary list one section at a time.

Preparation

Make a list of the vocabulary from the song that you want to teach. Decide how many groups to divide your class into and divide the vocabulary list into the same number

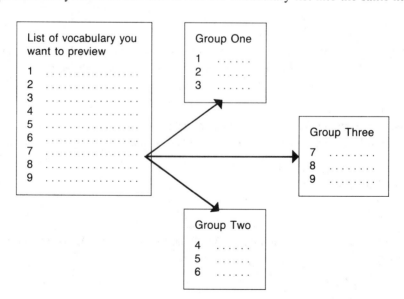

so that each group of students has part of the list. For example, if you want to work with nine vocabulary words and divide your class into three groups, each group would be given a slip of paper with three of the nine words.

In class

Give each group of students a different piece of paper with the vocabulary and ask them to write definitions for all the words any way they can, e.g. consulting with other students, asking the teacher, using their dictionaries. After a few minutes, give a signal and then pass the list to another group. Continue working and passing each list until each group has worked with each vocabulary list. Each group of students ends up with the list of vocabulary you originally gave them. In that way each group has a chance to contribute and/or change any of the definitions. While the vocabulary lists are being passed from group to group, you can have a look to monitor student progress.

When all groups have looked at all the vocabulary, go over each word as a whole class activity. Even if they were unable to get the correct definition, every student had a chance to look at and consider each word and will be very interested in your affirmation and/or correction. Remember that definitions should be appropriate to the song.

Links

For related techniques see **Vocabulary songs (7), Vocabulary association (9)** or **Making connections (29).**

7 Vocabulary songs

Secondary focus: listening

Song type: all songs

Level: very low to intermediate

Purpose: introducing or reviewing vocabulary

Students: adults and children

This technique can be used with any song to introduce or review vocabulary and idiomatic phrases.

Preparation

Write out the lyrics and have copies ready to hand out.

In class

Play the song with no preparation and no hand-outs. Tell the students to listen to the song and that you will give them the words in a minute. Then give the students the lyrics face down. When every student has a copy tell them to turn the lyrics over and play the song again. Tell them to listen to the song and circle any word or phrase they do not understand. Ask students to tell you what they circled. Discuss as a whole class or break into groups.

Extensions

1. Ask students to circle words that they *do* know. Ask the students to tell you or each other what the word means. Then listen again and with another coloured pen underline or circle words they do not know.

2. Write the vocabulary words or phrases on cards and save them for review.

3. Use the above cards for a Circle Conversation. Everybody sits in a circle. The

teacher turns over a card. One by one every student makes a sentence. No questions allowed. Either use the vocabulary directly in a sentence or use it as a theme. For example, if the word is 'love', students can make up a sentence which includes 'love' or can talk about something they love without necessarily including the word.

Links

For similar techniques see **Vocabulary association (9)** and **Punctuation (49).**

8 Alphabetical vocabulary

This exercise is quick and easy.

Preparation

Decide which words to review or introduce. Then list some or all the words alphabetically on a hand-out or write them on the board.

In class

Listen to the song once. Then listen again and ask students to number the words in the order in which they hear them. For example, the song *Row, Row, Row Your Boat* would look like this:

2	boat
5	dream
3	gently
1	row
4	stream

Links

For related techniques see **Song cards (20), Jumbled words (22), Did you hear it? (30)** and **More dictation (45).**

9 Vocabulary association

Secondary focus: discussion
writing

Song type: all songs

Level: intermediate

Purpose: word association

Students: adults

This technique works with vocabulary through word association. Individual words from a song are selected. Students are asked to list additional words that they associate to form word families. This helps students remember vocabulary in groups rather than as isolated units.

Preparation

Select a song and make a list of the vocabulary you want to work with. Sometimes it is helpful to select words that focus on a content theme or structures, e.g. nouns, adjectives, adverbs, prepositions or negatives.

In class

Make your vocabulary list available to students, for example, dictate the words for spelling practice. Then hand out the song lyrics. Listen to the song and ask students to circle the words in the lyrics from the list as they hear them sung. Then ask students to write two or three words they associate with each word on the original list. Finally, ask students to compare their lists and discuss.

Word from song	Example Associated Words
black	night, big, lost
give	present, like, action, ribbon

Extension

1. Pass out the lyric sheets and ask students to select the words they want to work with.

2. Draw a picture of the words and explain.

Links

For a related technique see **Drawing the song (2).**

10 Take it or leave it

Secondary focus:	listening
Song type:	all songs
Level:	very low to intermediate
Purpose:	enjoying songs
Students:	adults and children

Sometimes just providing a song and its lyrics with no task is enough to stimulate the natural curiosity of students.

Preparation

Select a popular song and write the lyrics. You may also want to provide a translation of the song in the students' L-1. If you have any special information about the song, tell the students: e.g. this song was number one in a given year or won a certain prize.

In class

Tell them you have no special reason for playing the song except that you thought that they might enjoy it. Then play the song at the end of class for listening only. Assign no homework or task of any kind. Hand out the lyrics as the students prepare to leave the class.

Links

For a related technique see **Song posters (48),** part 3.

11 Song word puzzles

Song type: all songs

Level: very low to intermediate

Purpose: word puzzle

Students: adults and children

Puzzles fascinate students, hold their attention and give a reason for working with language. The following technique is an easy way to make a puzzle.

Preparation

Select any word that has some connection with the theme of the song but is not in the lyrics. This is the secret word. Make as many lines in the puzzle as the secret word has letters. In the example below the secret word is 'California', which has ten letters. Therefore this puzzle has ten lines. Next, select ten words from the song. In the example below, the name of the song is 'San Francisco'. Each word you select must contain at least one letter from the secret word. Arrange the words so that the secret word can be seen after the puzzle is complete.

In class

Hand out the puzzle. Ask students to write in the answers and discover the secret word.

```
  1.  — — — — — — — c — — — —
                 2.  — a —
                 3.  — l — — —
                 4.  — i — — —
                     5.  f — —
                 6.  — o — —
                     7.  r — — —
  8.  — — — — — — — n
             9.  — — — i —
                 10.  — a —
```

Clues	*Answers*
1. city on the west coast of USA	San Francisco
2. large body of water	b*a*y
3. to be by yourself	a*l*one
4. moving air	w*i*ndy
5. can't see well in it	*f*og
6. where the heart is	h*o*me
7. where all reads lead to	*R*ome
8. when people don't think of me	forgotte*n*
9. a city with the nickname of 'city of light'	Par*i*s
10. not happy	s*a*d

What is the secret word? (California)

Hint

Render the word puzzle easier or more difficult by making the definitions more straightforward or more complicated.

Links

For related techniques see **Vocabulary association (9)** and **Definitions (14).**

12 Mistakes

Secondary focus: grammar
listening

Song type: all songs

Level: low to intermediate

Purpose: detecting mistakes

Students: adults and children

This is a technique which raises the consciousness of students about their mistakes and was inspired by the mistakes I found on record album lyric sheets.

Preparation

Think about common mistakes your students make such as spelling, singular and plural agreement, verb tenses, omitted and incorrect prepositions. Insert the mistakes in the lyric sheets you prepare for hand-outs.

In class

Hand out the lyric sheets containing the mistakes. Listen to the song and ask students to underline unusual, ungrammatical items or things that just don't make sense. Include some lines with no mistakes.

Extensions

1. Hand out the lyrics before you listen and ask the students to underline the mistakes. Discuss any mistakes the students find. Then play to verify or find additional mistakes.

2. Use this technique as an initial diagnostic test early in the semester. Include as many common mistakes as you can. Hand out the lyrics, but do not discuss them. Listen and ask students to underline. Count and tabulate the mistakes. This will give you an idea of what students can and cannot hear and where you might want

to work. Do the same song with the same lyric mistakes at the end of the semester to measure improvement.

Links

For similar techniques see **Song cards (20), The cloze passage (23)** and **Punctuation (49).**

13 Vocabulary competition

Secondary focus: listening
writing
discussion

Song type: all songs

Level: low to intermediate

Purpose: catching the lyrics

Students: adults

This is a good way to introduce a song and preview the vocabulary at the same time.

Preparation

No preparation is necessary.

In class

Divide the class into groups. Ask one person from each group to tell you one thing they like and use this as the name of their group. Ask students to get a pencil and a piece of paper handy. Tell them you are going to play the song once and their job is to write as many words as they can catch. Then play the song once only. Go from group to group asking for a word from the song, taking only one word from each group. Write the words on the board under the group name. Keep going around from group to group until they can give no more words. The group with the most words wins. The key to this technique is student motivation to win. After you

Name of group one e.g. Apples	Name of group two e.g. Purple Gloves	Name of group three e.g. Sports Cars
word from song listed here		

have as many words on the board as the students can provide, pass out the lyrics and listen again to confirm.

Links

For related techniques see **Word swatter (18), Did you hear it? (30)** and **Pop songs (32).**

14 Definitions

Secondary focus: listening

Song type: all songs

Level: very low to intermediate

Purpose: vocabulary definitions

Students: adults and children

This is a vocabulary exercise which makes the matching of words and definitions into a game.

Preparation

Write out the lyrics, select the vocabulary you want to test and write out definitions.

In class

If you have not worked with the song before, play it for general effect. Hand out the lyrics and deal with any vocabulary questions. Divide the class into pairs or teams. Read a simple definition of any word in the song; the first team to raise their hand can answer. The correct answer is the word in the song that fits the definition. Give one point for each correct answer. As an example, here are some definitions from the song *The Interview* from the ESL songbook *The Back Home Companion*. (For a list of ESL songbooks see the annotated bibliography on pages 160−2.)

Definitions	*Words in the song*
a very high hill	mountain
a very big, modern jet aircraft	jumbo jet
a person who flies an aeroplane	airline pilot

Links

For related techniques see **Vocabulary competition (13)**, **Word swatter (18)**, **Headlines (19)** and **Review quiz (28).**

15   Song poetry

Secondary focus: discussion

Song type: all songs

Level: low to intermediate

Purpose: focus poetic language

Students: adults and children

Songs contain many lines and phrases which are strikingly poetic. These lines can be matched with pictures to reinforce and expand the vocabulary.

Preparation

Gather some pictures, scissors, paste and large pieces of paper.

In class

Give students the lyrics, ask them to underline lines or phrases they like. Also give students some pictures, drawings, calendar art, etc. and ask them to match the song line with a picture they feel appropriate. Students can work in pairs, groups or the class as a whole to explain their selection. Paste the picture and song line on a large sheet of paper and post it on the wall or in the song corner. Below are some examples of songs, lines from the songs, and possible types of pictures that could be used to illustrate them. For song titles, performers and album numbers, see Index of songs mentioned in activities, page 173.

Song title	Song line	Types of pictures
Blue, Blue Ocean	'You're sailing out on a blue, blue sea'.	water, ocean, sailing, boats
Homeless	'Moonlight sleeping on a midnight lake'.	moonlight, lake, sleeping
	'Strong wind destroy our home'.	storm pictures

Song title	*Song line*	*Types of pictures*
	'Many dead, tonight it could be you'.	destruction, storms, car crashes, funerals
September Song	'When the autumn weather turns the leaves to flame . . .'	autumn trees, elderly people

Links

For related techniques see **Pictures (3), Song corner (38), Song posters (48), Picture selection (55), Feelings (58)** and **Clichés, proverbs and sayings (63).**

SECTION 2

LISTENING DEVELOPMENT

Introduction

Whereas the majority of the activities in this book will involve listening to a song, this section focuses on activities which will practise the skills of listening per se. These include detailed listening comprehension, listening for summarising or writing, listening to isolated vocabulary and listening for word order.

One overriding reason for using songs in language teaching is that students will far more willingly listen to a tape of a song than a dialogue or monologue. And they will listen with more attention in an attempt to catch the words. This section capitalises on this willingness.

16 Strip songs

Secondary focus:	discussion
Song type:	long songs
Level:	low to intermediate
Purpose:	jig-saw reading
Students:	adults and children

Preparation

Cut the song lyrics into strips.

In class

Hand out the strips to students in pairs or groups and ask them to arrange them *before* they listen. For higher classes, ask students to discuss why they arranged the strips as they did. What clues helped them? Story development? Transition words? Finally, listen and rearrange strips as necessary.

Extensions

1. Give one strip to each student, ask the student to memorise the strip and throw it away. Then ask the students to arrange themselves in what they believe to be the correct order. When they have arranged themselves, recite the song to the class.

2. Paste the strips on a sheet of coloured paper and put on the bulletin board. See **Song posters (48)**.

3. Continue working with the song using techniques **Definitions (14)** and then extended **Discussion questions (57)** or **Point of view (59)**.

Links

For additional lesson plan suggestions involving long songs (either fast or slow) see Appendix: Sample lesson plans and selected songs, pages 163–6.

17 Tell them a story

Secondary focus: discussion
writing

Song type: songs that tell stories

Level: low to intermediate

Purpose: introducing a song

Students: adults and children

This is a listening technique that provides students with a paraphrased version of the song before they hear it. It is especially good for introducing songs that tell stories because it gives students the story line before they listen to the actual song.

Preparation

Write out the words to the song. Then write a paraphrased version for your class.

In class

Read the paraphrased version of the song to your students. This example comes from the song *Rudolph the Red-nosed Reindeer*.

Rudolph was a reindeer who lived in the north land where there is a lot of snow and ice. He was normal or usual-looking except for his nose. He was the only reindeer with a red nose. In fact, his nose would shine and glow in the dark. At night he could always see because of his nose. But the other reindeer didn't like Rudolph because his nose made him look different. They laughed at him. Also they would not let him play games with them.

Then one December night something unusual happened. It was very foggy and Santa Claus could not see. When Santa and his regular reindeer flew into the sky they became lost because they could not see any lights, roads or landmarks. So Santa went to Rudolph and asked him to help him. Santa asked Rudolph to be the lead reindeer. In other words, Rudolph would be in front and the light from his nose would give enough light for Santa and the other reindeer to see. In that way, they would be able to fly to give presents to girls and boys around the world.

After Santa and the reindeer returned to Rudolph's home town, Rudolph was a hero. All the other reindeer were proud of him and said that everybody in the world would always remember him.

Paraphrases can be written using easier language for lower classes or more difficult language for higher classes. As an optional step, hand out the story for silent reading and class discussion. Finally, listen to the song and hand out the song lyrics if desired.

Extensions

1. Consider the song a snapshot. Ask students to make up the background. What happened to bring these people to the point of the song?

2. Instead of a paraphrase, write a short summary.

Links

After introducing the song with this activity, you can continue with **Strip songs (16)** and **Point of view (59)**, both of which work with any song that tells a story. For suggested lesson plans using songs that tell stories, see Appendix: Sample lesson plans and selected songs, pages 163–6.

18 Word swatter

Secondary focus: vocabulary

Song type: all songs, especially fast songs

Level: very low to low intermediate

Purpose: word recognition

Students: adults and children

This is a game which can be used either to preview or review vocabulary items.

Preparation

Decide on the vocabulary and write each word or phrase on a card.

In class

Put the cards on the table and play the song. Students hit the words when they hear the word and then pick them up. The student or team with the most cards wins.

Variations

Buy or make a word swatter (like a fly swatter, only for words) for each student or team. Students can work individually, in pairs, or in teams. One student swats, then hands the swatter to another member of the team. If a competitive game is desired, make one set of cards. If a non-competitive game is desired, make several sets of cards.

Links

For related techniques see **Did you hear it? (30)** or **Song cards (20).**

19 Headlines

Secondary focus:	discussion
Song type:	all songs
Level:	low to intermediate
Purpose:	relating headlines to lyrics
Students:	adults

Preparation

Select a song and cut out newspaper headlines which illustrate the theme.

In class

Explain vocabulary and idioms. Then put the newspaper headlines on a table. Play the song and tell the students to pick up the headlines when they hear them. If possible, ask students to explain the relationship of the headline to the song.

Links

Other techniques with a similar orientation are **Word swatter (18), Vocabulary association (9)** and **Title matchings (27).**

20 Song cards

Secondary focus: singing

Song type: short and slow songs

Level: very low to low intermediate

Purpose: jig-saw reading

Students: adults and children

Song cards are blank cards on which the teacher writes the words to the song. Each card has a single word or phrase written on it. Together all the cards form the complete set of lyrics. While listening, the students arrange the cards in order. This activity works very well with short, slow songs but not fast songs because students do not have enough time to move the cards. Below are four cards for the Christmas song, *Silent Night*.

Silent	Night
All is	calm

Preparation

Buy some cards about the size of business cards or cut a larger card into smaller pieces. Paper works as well, but a card lasts longer and is easier to handle. Write all the words to the song on the cards. For a very short song put one word on one card.

In class

Play the song through once to give a preview. Tell the students to listen only and not to take notes because you are going to show them the words. Put the cards face up on a table or flat surface. One set of cards can be used by several students. Play the song and ask the students to arrange the cards in correct order. This typically takes at least three listenings.

Use song cards for review in a later lesson and the challenge and interest will remain high. Song cards are very successful because they use several sense modalities: the visual, the auditory and the kinaesthetic. Even students who only listen and watch while other students put the cards in order are participating through their visual and auditory senses.

Extensions

1. Song cards are a good way to introduce singing. After several sessions of working with song cards, the tune as well as the words become very familiar.

2. Select the concrete nouns and draw a picture on a card instead of the word; insert in the deck or use as a quiz.

3. Paste the cards on a large piece of paper and hang on the wall. See **Song posters (48).**

4. Use song cards to review a song introduced by another technique such as **Vocabulary songs (7).**

5. Ask students to arrange song cards before they listen.

Hint

For a complete lesson plan for a short, slow song for a low-level class see Appendix: Sample lesson plans and selected songs, pages 163–6.

21 Structure review

Secondary focus:	writing discussion
Song type:	all songs
Level:	very low to low
Purpose:	grammar cloze
Students:	adults and children

Songs can be used as a natural and interesting way to review almost any grammatical point.

Preparation

Decide which grammar or structural points you want to practise, e.g. verb tenses, singular/plural forms, prepositions, articles. Select a song that has the points you wish to review. Prepare the song lyrics with the review points clozed. For information on clozing passages see **The cloze passage (23)** or **Grammar letter (51)**.

In class

To sensitise students to the teaching point, play the song and ask the students to count the number of times they heard the review point. Hand out the song lyrics with a cloze of the points. Ask students to fill in the cloze *before* listening, then listen to confirm. Alternatively, fill in the cloze while listening.

Extensions

1. Ask students to underline contractions or reduced forms, then give the full form.

2. Practise listening comprehension with contractions (I'll, we'll) or sounds (R and L). It is possible to work on more than one point at the same time.

Hint

Number the blank spaces in the cloze exercise (put a small number under each clozure). This makes it easy to reference the line especially when you are asking the students to read them back.

Links

For related techniques see **Grammar letter (51)** and **Mistakes (12).**

22 Jumbled words

Song type: short and slow songs

Level: very low to low

Purpose: arranging word order

Students: adults and childen

This technique gives all the words but in jumbled order.

Preparation

Write the words on the board or prepare a hand-out as in the example below. Below are the words for the song *Row, Row, Row Your Boat*.

	dream	down	row	but	the	
merrily	row	boat	stream	gently		merrily
a	your	is	row	merrily	life	merrily

In class

Ask students to listen and write the lyrics.

Hint

As they listen, ask students to circle any word they do not understand.

Links

For related techniques see **Dictation (44), More dictation (45)** or **Alphabetical vocabulary (8).**

23 The cloze passage

Secondary focus:	grammar
Song type:	short and slow songs
Level:	very low to intermediate
Purpose:	cloze
Students:	adults and children

A cloze passage is any written material with every nth word blanked out. It is the most familiar and popular song activity currently used and, for that reason, is probably over-used.

Preparation

Prepare your hand-out or write on the board. For example, if you decided to blank out every fifth word of the song *My Country Tis of Thee* (tune: *God Save the Queen*) it would look like this.

> My country tis of _____
> Sweet land of liberty,
> _____ thee I sing

with the missing or blanked-out words being 'thee' and 'of'.

    An alternative to blanking out every nth word is to blank out a teaching point, e.g. blank out the prepositions. This focuses the cloze in the direction you want. Another option is to cloze out the stressed and easy-to-hear words rather than contractions, prepositions or other hard-to-catch words. The important thing in using a cloze passage is to be aware of what you are clozing out and why.

In class

Listen to the song and then hand out the cloze song lyrics. Ask students to listen until they are able to fill in all the blanks or give up. Verify the correct words. At this point, you can stop or move to another technique. See Appendix: Sample lesson plans and selected songs, pages 163–6 for two suggested lesson plans using a cloze passage with short, slow songs.

Suggestions

1. Ask students to work in pairs.

2. Give students additional help, such as the first letter of every clozed word. For example, 'Country r _____, take me home'.

3. Anticipation. Ask students to write in what they think might go in the blanks before they listen. Stress that they should guess even if they are not sure.

4. Avoid clozing two or three words in a row as students usually cannot catch them and you will have to stop the tape and/or replay the tape several times. Cloze only one word per line.

5. If you want to use the same cloze hand-out for more than one class, number the clozed passages and ask students to write the words on a separate piece of paper.

24 All-purpose questions

Secondary focus: grammar
discussion

Song type: all songs

Level: very low to intermediate

Purpose: questions

Students: adults and children

This collection of questions is divided into pre-listening questions, while-listening questions, and follow-up questions. These questions can be used to:

1. introduce a song,

2. quiz students on their reaction to a song,

3. gauge their grasp of content, or

4. work on grammar points such as future and past tenses.

Preparation

Look at the questions below and decide which ones to use. Be selective, do not try to use them all. Tell the students the name of the song and any additional information you know that you feel might be helpful. Then ask the questions, write them on the board, or pass them out. Play the song and discuss the answers.

Pre-listening questions

1. What type of music do you think this song will be? Rock, country, folk, etc.
2. Do you expect the singer will be man/woman; over thirty/under thirty; US, British, etc.
3. Is this song going to be happy or sad?
4. Will the song be fast, moderate or slow?
5. What are some of the words you expect to hear?

6. In one word or phrase, what is this song going to be about?
7. Do you think you are going to like this song?

While-listening questions

(These questions must be based on the actual lyrics of the song.)

1. Tick (√) all the . . .
2. Write down all the . . .
3. Answer these true/false questions.
4. Count the times you hear . . .
5. Did you hear _____ or _____?
6. Listen and tell me who, what, when, where, why, did, is, are . . .

Follow-up questions

 1. What kind of music was this?
 2. How did you feel while you listened?
 3. What did you think about while you listened?
 4. What words do you remember now?
 5. Would you like to listen again? Why or why not?
 6. Would you like to listen to another song by the same singer or group?
 7. Did you notice how you moved your body when you listened?
 8. How would you describe this music?
 9. Have you ever heard this song before? This type of song? Where?
10. What do you think the singer/group looks like?
11. If you had to give this song a new title, what would it be?
12. What happened in the composer's life to make him/her write this?
13. What is one word (in this song) that best describes it?
14. What is the one word or what are some words (not in the song) that best describes it?

Links

For related techniques that ask questions see **Vocabulary prediction (1)** or **Discussion questions (57)**. See also **Multiple choice (60)** for a technique that is designed for instrumental music but could also be used for pop songs.

25 BGM (background music)

Secondary focus:	discussion writing
Song type:	instrumental music
Level:	very low to intermediate
Purpose:	mood setting
Students:	adults and children

BGM is any music played while the students are doing something else and not paying full attention to the music.

Preparation

Select some music suitable for the purpose of BGM. The music should not be noticeable or draw attention to itself. Avoid music which has a wide dynamic range (moves from very high to low pitch). Generally, do not use music with words unless the words are soft or in a language students do not know. Sudden music jars students and draws attention to itself. To avoid this, put the tape in your player and then turn the volume down. Push the play button and slowly turn up the volume.

In class

BGM can be used in language classrooms in a variety of ways.

Masking

This is the most common use of BGM and is used in such places as coffee shops and restaurants to give a feeling of privacy. Play BGM any time the students are working silently, writing or involved in group discussions.

Mood setting

Play BGM either before or after class to set the mood of the class. I saw this done very effectively at the Cambridge English School in Tokyo where senior instructor

Tom Hinton played a Palestrina tape about ten minutes before his advanced class began. He came into the classroom early, wrote the name of the composer and music on the board, turned on the cassette player and left the room.

Mood changing

This was developed by musical therapists working in hospitals who noticed that music with a fast tempo had the effect of increasing the heartbeat and music with a slow tempo tended to lower the heartbeat. For a tired evening class that you would like to liven up, find a blank tape and record a few minutes of slow music, then a few minutes of moderate tempo music and finally some fast music. Reversing this process has the opposite effect.

Song preview

Play a song as BGM that you want to use in the future so students become familiar with it in an indirect way. Play the song before a class, after a class or during a transition period.

Exercise timing

Make a pre-timed tape of BGM with silence at both ends. For example, to time a reading passage of three minutes make a tape of quiet, reading music. If you have a favourite song that is not distracting or a short instrumental piece, play it through and time it. In class tell the students that they have about x minutes or until the song is finished to complete the exercise, pair work discussion, etc.

Cocktail party

This BGM game uses party music while students stand up and mingle around the room practising introductions, openers, closers, dialogues or grammar structures just studied. Select any instrumental music that you feel provides a pleasant but lively background.

Reading

Use music as background for reading a poem or a story to the class.

Creative writing

Music can also be used as background for creative writing. Select and play long selections of music such as Tchaikowsky's Piano Concerto No. 1 and Gershwin's 'Rhapsody in Blue'. Ask students to write a poem or prose response to the music and their feelings. For another approach to the use of music as a stimulus for writing see **Movies in your mind (50)**.

Links

For other techniques using instrumental music see **Theme music (52), Song strings (54), Picture selection (55), Multiple choice (60)** and **Sound quiz (74).**

26 The top twenty

Song type: long songs

Level: very low to intermediate

Purpose: ordering top-twenty songs

Students: adults

This is a listening exercise for students who are interested in top-twenty popular songs. It is also a way for teachers to become familiar with current top pops.

Preparation

Record a disc jockey (DJ) reading the top-twenty songs or record it yourself. Then make a hand-out of the top-twenty songs in order but put the names of the recording artists in random order:

20.	Name of song	_____	Tina Turner
19.	Name of song	_____	Eurythmics
18.	. . . .	. . . .	
	. . . .	. . . .	
1.	Name of song	_____	Culture Club

In class

Divide the students into groups or teams. Then hand out the top-twenty list. Tell the students that they will listen to a tape of a DJ giving the top-twenty songs and the singers or groups that perform them. Their job is to write the number of the song by the singer or group. For example, the voice on the tape will say 'number twenty by so and so'. The students put a twenty in front of so and so's name. Tell the students to stand up while listening. When they have finished the task, the group can sit down. This is a pressure point which motivates action.

Links

For a related technique using pressure points see **Definitions (14)**. For another way of dealing with top-twenty pop songs see **Pop songs (32)** and **Discussion questions (57)**.

27 Title matchings

Secondary
focus: discussion

Song type: all songs

Level: low to intermediate

Purpose: matching titles to songs

Students: adults

Titles of songs frequently relate directly to the theme of a song and are usually part of the lyrics. Ask students to listen to a short extract from a song and to guess the title. This encourages students to make intelligent guesses based on contextual clues.

Preparation

Select five songs that your students may or may not know but that you have *not* studied in class. Also make a list of ten song titles, five of which are the actual titles of songs you have selected and five additional titles.

In class

Give the students the list of ten titles. Play a short extract from each song; ask the students to listen and make their best guess at the correct title. If the students like one song in particular, that can be the next song to study.

Hints

1. You may have to teach your students how to recognise contextual clues such as rhyme schemes.

2. Do not play the chorus or any portion of the lyrics which contains the title.

3. Make a composite tape made up of parts of the five songs.

Links

For related techniques see **Headlines (19)** and **Jacket covers (70)**. For an opposite technique that makes matching titles and lyrics into a test, see **Review quiz (28).**

28   Review quiz

Song type: all songs

Level: very low to intermediate

Purpose: matching titles to songs

Students: adults and children

Preparation

Make a list of all the songs you have used during the semester. Hand-out 1 is an example of a list of titles and artists and hand-out 2 is an example of a list of song lyrics.

Hand-out number 1	Hand-out number 2
1. . . . . 2. Mary Had a Little Lamb 3. 4. etc.	a. it followed her to school one day. b. . . . . c. . . . . d. . . . . etc. . . . .

In class

Give both hand-outs to the students or write them on the board. Then ask students to write the name of the song (from hand-out 1) next to the words (on hand-out 2). To verify you can give the correct answer or play the songs.

Hints

1. If convenient, combine song titles and song lines on the same page.

2. Ask students to write the name of the song title and/or performer on hand-out number 2. Note the blank line for that purpose in number a of hand-out 2. Or ask students to write just numbers 1, 2, 3, etc.

Links

For an opposite technique see **Title matchings (27).**

29　Making connections

Secondary focus:　vocabulary

Song type:　slow songs

Level:　very low to low

Purpose:　collocations

Students:　adults and children

This is a task-oriented, listening exercise that requires very little preparation.

Preparation

Make two lists of words, both from the same song. Indicate one list by using numbers and indicate the other list by using the alphabet.

In class

Hand out the two lists, write them on the board or dictate them. Play the song and ask students to draw a line from a word on the first list to a word on the second list. The two words or phrases should follow each other on the same line in the song. Below is an example from the song *Clementine*.

1. Oh my　　　　　a. sorry
2. lost　　　　　　b. gone forever
3. dreadful　　　　c. darling

Links

For related techniques see **Jumbled words (22)** and **Did you hear it? (30).**

30 Did you hear it?

**Secondary
focus:**   vocabulary

Song type: all songs

Level: very low to low intermediate

Purpose: intensive listening

Students: adults and children

This is a very simple to prepare exercise that asks students to distinguish between what they did hear and what they did not hear.

Preparation

List some words from a song, e.g. key vocabulary or structure words. Keep the words in the same order as in the song. In other words, list words from the first part of the song first and list words from the middle and end of the song later. This makes it easier to follow and find the words. Be sure to add several distracters sprinkled throughout the list which sound very close to items in the song to encourage close discrimination.

In class

After students have the list, play the song and ask students to circle or check the word on the list if they hear it.

Extension

1. Instead of listing key vocabulary, list grammatical structures (e.g. prepositions, verbs), events that happened in the song or sounds (e.g. all words beginning with an /r/ or containing an /r/ sound).

2. On the board write sentences such as 'Could you say that again, please?' and 'How do you spell it?' Then dictate the word list to the students, making sure

you say the words in a normal way and not clearly or slowly. The point is to encourage students to ask you for help.

Links

For related techniques see **Word swatter (18), Song cards (20)** and **Jumbled words (22).**

31 Titles

Secondary focus: writing

Song type: all songs

Level: intermediate

Purpose: listening for gist

Students: adults

This activity could be used to introduce a song.

Preparation

No special preparation is necessary.

In class

Tell students they will listen to a song and that after they listen you will ask them to write a sentence about the meaning. Also tell them that you will ask them to write a title for the song. Play the song then ask students to write a sentence on the meaning of the song. Share in groups or the whole class. Now ask students to write what they think could be a good title. Share in groups or the whole class.

Links

For related techniques see **Headlines (19)**, **Title matchings (27)** and **Review quiz (28)**. Also see **Paraphrasing (43)** for working with meaning.

32 Pop songs: when words are impossible to catch

Song type: long, fast songs

Level: low to intermediate

Purpose: dealing with hard to catch lyrics

Students: adults and children

Many popular songs are sung in such a way that the words are difficult to catch, but it is often just this kind of music that students most want to listen to. Rather than only using slow and easy to understand music in your classroom, this technique makes it possible to play music with difficult to catch lyrics.

Preparation

Obtain the full lyrics of the song and prepare them to be handed out.

In class

Step 1. Listen to the song with no text or preparation. The student's level of understanding will be close to zero. Ask what words they could catch.

Step 2. Play the song again but this time read a line before playing the song. In other words, read a line and play a line. Students will not understand all the vocabulary nor will they retain much in long-term memory, but they will understand and recognise that what you are saying is indeed what is being sung.

Step 3. Pass out the full text and ask the students to listen again while they are looking at the lyrics. In three short, simple steps you have taken the students from almost zero to full understanding. Finally, discuss vocabulary, idioms, grammar and any other questions.

Extensions

1. In step 3, instead of passing out the full lyrics, pass out a clozed form of the lyrics. You have many options as to how much to cloze. For a low class, cloze easy

to catch words; for a slightly higher class, cloze full phrases or every fifth word. For a high class give only the first two or three words in each sentence. See **The cloze passage (23)**.

2. After completing step 3, ask the students to turn the complete lyrics over, listen and fill in a clozed passage. You will have to decide how many times to listen. Then compare their cloze lyrics and the full lyrics that you gave them previously. Students will be able to see for themselves what words and phrases they cannot hear.

Links

Continue working with the song with techniques such as **Dialogue drama (47), Discussion questions (57)** or **Point of view (59).**

33   Rhythm and stress

Song type: all songs

Level: very low to intermediate

Purpose: practising stress and rhythm

Students: adults and children

Songs contain the rhythm of language and can be used to sensitise students to rhythm and stress and thus help pronunciation. This is especially helpful for students who speak a syllable timed language when they are studying a stress timed language such as English.

Preparation

Select a song and prepare the lyrics.

In class

Hand out the lyrics. Ask students to listen to the song while looking at the lyrics and put a pencil mark over the word when they hear the stress. Check their work by saying the words with exaggerated stress. After students have made any changes, ask them to work in pairs. Ask one student to snap his/her fingers or hit the desk with a pencil in time to the stress marks while the other student says the lyrics, keeping the same time.

Links

For related techniques see **Rhyme after rhyme (5), Breathing easy (36)** and **Strike up the band (39).**

34 Two versions

Secondary focus: writing

Song type: all songs

Level: very low to intermediate

Purpose: comparing versions of songs

Students: adults

It is not uncommon for certain songs to be recorded by several singers. Usually these versions differ and these differences can provide a listening task.

Preparation

Find two versions of a song.

In class

Hand out the lyrics, play one version of the song and discuss. Then play another version of the song. For lower-level students, ask them to underline where they heard differences. For higher-level students, ask them to write the difference.

Links

For related techniques see **Mistakes (12)** and **Song competition (68).**

35 Lists

Secondary focus: writing
                       discussion
                       grammar

Song type: all songs

Level: very low to intermediate

Purpose: classifying vocabulary

Students: adults and children

Many song lyrics mention objects or a sequence of events. A simple but effective exercise is to ask students to list the items or events. For a beginner class you can stop at this point but for a higher class you can continue with a discussion by applying the list to the students' lives.

Preparation

Find a song that lists a series of events or things. Write the list for your reference. Below are some examples; see Index of songs mentioned in activities, page 173 for singer and album numbers: *Reelin' and Rockin'* mentions times; *Big River* mentions cities; *When Numbers Get Serious* mentions numbers and mathematical terms; *Moonlight in Vermont* mentions things in winter scene; *These Foolish Things* mentions objects that remind singer of her/his lover.

In class

Ask students to listen and to list the events or objects they hear. If they are objects, students can rank them; if they are times, students can list them in order or list what the singer was doing at each time. Then personalise the list. For example, if the song contained several things to drink, students could describe their favourite drink; if the song contained several times, students could tell what they do at those times or give their daily schedule.

Extension

Instead of listing events in the song, ask students to list grammatical structures. Then personalise the list; for example, select the nouns they like, what verbs they have done or want to do.

Links

See **All-purpose questions (24)** or **Did you hear it? (30).**

36   Breathing easy

Song type: long songs

Level: very low to intermediate

Purpose: practising breath groups

Students: adults and children

Many students are unaware of the natural breath patterns of English. This technique gives practice in identifying and listening for natural breath patterns.

Preparation

Prepare the song lyrics, but do not include any punctuation. Read through the lyrics marking the natural breath groups or ask a colleague to mark it for you. Asking a colleague to note the breath groups allows you to bring in a third opinion and avoid confronting your students with a 'my perfect opinion against your imperfect opinion' situation.

In class

Write the first line of the song on the board and use it to explain breath groups. You might ask a student to come to the board and mark it by putting slash marks like these /xxx/xxx/ to mark the breath groups. Hand out the lyrics and, if this is a new song, go over vocabulary, idioms etc. Before they listen ask students to draw a line marking the natural breath groups. After they are finished you might ask one or two of them to read a sentence or verse of the lyrics as they have marked them. Then listen to the song to confirm or change.

Hint

Ask students to use one colour pen or pencil when first marking and another colour when listening so they can see the differences more clearly.

Links

For related techniques see **Rhyme after rhyme (5), Rhythm and stress (33)** or **Punctuation (49).**

37 Scrambled lyrics

Secondary focus: vocabulary

Song type: short songs

Level: very low to intermediate

Purpose: recognising and ordering lyrics

Students: adults and children

This technique is good with short songs with simple lyrics. Whether the song is fast or slow does not make as much difference.

Preparation

Make a special hand-out of the lyrics as shown below.

In class

Preteach any difficult or new vocabulary. Give the hand-out to the students. Listen and order the lyrics in the correct order by writing the sequence in the circles. Number 1 is marked.

Links

Continue working with the song by using other techniques such as **All-purpose questions (24)**, **Making connections (29)**, **Grammar letter (51)** or **Song competition (68)**.

38 Song corner

Secondary focus: writing
discussion

Song type: all songs

Level: very low to intermediate

Purpose: classroom management

Students: adults and children

Assign one section or corner of your classroom for the purpose of song and music activity. Keep your tape players and class tapes there so students can go there in their free time.

Possible uses

1. Find a bookcase or table that fits the song corner. Keep your tape player and some tapes there. When the time comes for a song or music activity, direct the class towards the corner. If headphones are available, students can listen in their free time.

2. Along the top of the wall where students can easily see, put up quotes about songs and music, for example a proverb such as 'music is the eye of the ear'. Additional quotations on the subject of music include:

    '... music utters the things that cannot be spoken' (Ashley Montague).

    'Give me the making of the songs of a nation and I care not who makes its laws.'

    'If music be the food of love, play on' (Shakespeare, *Twelfth Night,* Act I, scene 1).

    'Music is the food of love' (Proverb, probably based on Shakespeare).

    'The reed-player of your own street does not charm' (Egyptian proverb).

'Music has charms to soothe a savage breast' (William Congreve, *The Mourning Bride*, Act I, scene 1).

'The Voice is the best music' (proverb)

'We are the music-makers,
and we are the dreamers of dreams ...
Yet we are the movers and shakers
Of the world for ever, it seems' (Arthur O'Shaughnessy, 1874).

3. Put up a paper where students can request songs they want to hear.

4. If paper or copy facilities are in short supply, write song lyrics on brown paper or even newsprint, which can be taped to the wall.

Links

For related techniques, see **Song posters (48), Song poetry (15)** and **Jacket covers (70).**

SECTION 3

SINGING
DEVELOPMENT

Introduction

Singing a song, however simple, in another language is a pleasing achievement even for people who do not sing much in their own language. This short section will suggest activities to encourage the singing of the song you have chosen, and may be used in addition to many activities in the rest of the book.

Many teachers have made observations about singing and what follows is a compilation of hints and recommendations.

1. Students must hear the song all the way through before they attempt to sing it. For more on this see **Human tape recorder (42)**.

2. Do not sing the difficult lines slowly. Rather, sing the whole song slowly at first, gradually increasing speed to normal.

3. Do not teach a song with a number of verses in one lesson. Teach one verse per lesson.

4. When learning a song, the teacher should sing the whole song with the students instructed to join in, gradually replacing the teacher in those parts that the students can hear and understand, for example the refrain.

5. Part singing for songs can be done by dividing the phrases of the song among two or more students: a soloist and a chorus; a different soloist for each verse with a chorus for the refrain; or boys and girls.

6. The students can begin to sing the song with la la la or lu lu lu for the words until the melody is learned.

7. Students can repeat the words in rhythmic word groups. In that way they practise saying the words in the same way they will sing them. Another way is to hum the melody first, then chant the rhythm and finally sing.

8. It restores energy to ask the students to stand while singing, especially if most other activities have been sitting.

9. Limit Christmas songs to a few carols. Start learning these carols early enough in the year so that they can be used all through the holiday season.

10. To deal with shyness and reluctance to sing, ask students to stand in a circle and face out rather than in so as to avoid eye contact. In other words, sing to the wall.

11. Designate a song for each unit of your text. Sing your theme or unit song at the end of the class/week for review. Sing it at the end of the semester party.

12. Develop a singing period in your class: every day or two or three times a week.

Sing to begin or end a class or to separate two distinct topics. Even ten minutes a day will help.

13. Using a tape recorder: after students can sing a song well, record them. This will come in handy if you do not have a commercial tape of a song or you want an easy sing-along recording.

39   Strike up the band

Song type: any singable song

Level: very low to intermediate

Purpose: developing a sense of rhythm

Students: adults and children

Listening to songs and singing songs can be helpful to second language learners as they strive to develop the rhythm pattern of the new language. This activity generates enough noise to mask any initial embarrassment of singing.

Preparation

No special preparation is necessary.

In class

Introduce the song by some technique such as **Vocabulary songs (7), Song cards (20)** or **Jumbled words (22)**. Then ask students to find something that makes a noise and practise using it. Some suggestions are: hand clapping, finger snapping; hands hitting on desk, book, or other objects; using a pencil or pen to tap desk or table; hitting two pencils or pens together; tapping a cassette case or pencil case with ruler or pencil. Practise some of the above sounds and encourage your students to invent new sound makers. Select a sound maker yourself and demonstrate the rhythm of the song. Sing the song yourself and usually students will join you without much urging.

Links

For related techniques see **Rhyme after rhyme (5), Rhythm and stress (33)** and **Breathing easy (36).**

40 Mini musicals

Secondary focus:	discussion
	writing
Song type:	any singable song
Level:	very low to intermediate
Purpose:	performing a musical
Students:	adults and children

A mini musical is a performance that has some sort of theme, contains some singing and some spoken dialogue. Songs can be grouped to create your own mini musical and be performed for the class, for other classes, for a whole school programme, holiday parties or for parents' groups.

Preparation

Select a theme for your musical. Consult your textbook or ask the class. Select three to five songs. The songs need to be singable, but you can use only part of a song, for example, one or two verses or even a chorus instead of the whole song. Do not forget to look at ESL songbooks as well as pop music. See pages 160−2 for a list of ESL songbooks. If the students like a song that is too difficult to sing, students could mime. Also consider English translations of well-known local songs, children's songs and folk songs.

In class

Either you or the class write all the spoken dialogues to introduce and connect the story line. Special groups might be set up for this task. There are several options in singing. You can have solo parts, duets, trios, quartets, a chorus, or antiphonal singing between chorus and a smaller group. You can also have audience singing. Lastly consider props, costumes and scenery. Once you have rehearsed, go on tour by visiting other classrooms or perform for the whole school.

41 Singing with a little help from my friends

Song type: any singable song

Level: very low to intermediate

Purpose: encouraging students to sing

Students: adults and children

This technique gives students support in singing a song for the first time.

Preparation

Select a song and deal with the vocabulary. If the song has several verses, begin singing only one. Do not overload your students. You can sing the others later.

In class

Write the verse on the board and number the lines. The teacher sings the whole verse. If the song has four lines, the teacher sings the first three lines and asks the students to sing line four as s/he sings it. Then the teacher sings lines one and two by her/himself and asks the students to join in, singing lines three and four. Then the teacher sings line one and students sing lines two, three and four. Finally students sing the whole verse.

Extension

Instead of singing, you can say, chant or clap the verse.

Links

See **Human tape recorder (42)** as well as the tips listed in the introduction to this section.

42 Human tape recorder

Song type: singable songs

Level: very low to intermediate

Purpose: encouraging students to sing

Students: adults and children

How can a teacher get reluctant students to sing? A human voice is often better than a tape recorder for this purpose. With your own voice you can raise or lower the pitch of any song to a comfortable singing zone and you can stop and start at any place. Your own voice is also the best demonstration of singing possibility. If the teacher can sing, anybody can.

Preparation

Consider the problems involved in getting students to sing. For you, the teacher, the problem is how to get them to sing. For the students, the problem is how to match a strange tune with new words. The solution to the problem is for you to sing the song to allow the students to hear the words in the context of the tune.

Be sure you are confident to sing the song in front of the class all the way through. The problem will not be your voice as much as it will be that about halfway through the song you may begin to feel lonely. One of the reasons for this feeling of abandonment is that you will notice that your students are not looking at you and encouraging your heroic efforts, but looking down at the song lyrics. The temptation for you will be to stop singing and in a hurt, self-righteous tone of voice inform them that they are supposed to be singing. Avoid this temptation. Give them more time to absorb the relation of the words to the music.

In class

Invite your students to join you in singing as soon as they feel they can. Sing the song or verse all the way through, knowing that probably the first time none of them will join you. Then sing it again and probably one or two may join you or at least start to move their lips. By the third time they will join you. If they do not, stop, because there is a problem, e.g. the students do not want to sing, cannot sing, do not feel comfortable with the words, etc.

SECTION 4

WRITING
DEVELOPMENT

Introduction

Apart from writing down the lyrics there are many ways to exploit songs for writing practice. Songs that tell a story or even those that do not quite often suggest a narrative that can be written down, and many pieces of music without words convey dramatic narrative to the imagination. In this section the activities will suggest various ways of getting your students to write, inspired by songs and music.

43 Paraphrasing

Secondary focus:	discussion
Song type:	long songs
Level:	intermediate
Purpose:	summarising and paraphrasing
Students:	adults

In addition to providing authentic input, songs are long enough and complex enough to provide material for the practice necessary to develop the skill of paraphrasing.

Preparation

Write out the lyrics and then write a paraphrased version of the song. Your paraphrased version may be a line-for-line paraphrase or a short paragraph.

In class

Introduce the song. If you have worked with the song before, just listen. If not, introduce it by using another technique, for example **Strip songs (16), The cloze passage (23)** or **Vocabulary songs (7)**. Hand out the lyrics and your paraphrase. Ask students to select the paraphrase they think best. Discuss why.

Paraphrasing is a necessary discussion and clarification tool, but it is not easy. It is rather difficult to paraphrase a thought or an idea without changing its meaning and many otherwise competent English speakers — including a few teachers — have trouble doing it.

1. It is used to check and verify understanding.

2. It must be in the students' own words and they cannot use the same key words from the original, e.g. the phrase 'somewhere over the rainbow' cannot be paraphrased as 'above the rainbow' but might be paraphrased as 'somewhere far away' or 'in the land of dreams'.

3. A paraphrase is not an opinion or an interpretation. It must reflect the original meaning. It tends, however, to use simpler words than the original.

4. A paraphrase is usually introduced by a phrase such as:

    in other words . . .
    are you saying (that) . . .
    do you mean . . .
    so what you're saying is . . .

Extensions

1. Write a paraphrase of some of the lines of the song and mix these with the remaining original lines. Students arrange in correct order.

2. Write out a line-by-line paraphrase, reproduce it and cut it into strips. Students arrange the paraphrased strips in correct order either by listening to the song or by comparing the paraphrased strips with the original lyrics.

3. Rewrite street language or dialects into standard language. Ask students to identify and match.

4. Students work in groups. One group writes a paraphrased version of the odd lines, another group writes a paraphrased version of the even lines. They then change, correct and rewrite.

5. Assign all the lines from a song, one line to each student or pair or group. Ask each working group to write a paraphrase of their line. After each group has finished writing their paraphrased line, have the lines read in correct order. If you want, paste the line on coloured paper and post next to the original lyrics. See **Song posters (48)**.

Links

Continue this activity with a discussion technique such as **Discussion questions (57)** or **Values (65)**.

44 Dictation

**Secondary
focus:**   listening
               singing

Song type: short and slow songs

Level: very low to low intermediate

Purpose: lyrics as dictation

Students: adults and children

Preparation

Select an appropriate song.

In class

Give the students the tape and tape player. Tell them to play the tape as many times as they want until they can write the words to the song.

Hints

1. Decide whether you will allow the students to stop the tape in the middle of the song or whether they should play it all the way through before rewinding.

2. The key to success in dictation is the selection of an appropriate song. The problem is that you never know until you try.

3. Set a time limit or assign dictation for homework.

4. Dictation is a good way to introduce a song, especially for singing. After listening many times, students will have not only the words but the melody.

5. As a last step give students a copy of the lyrics to compare and self-correct their versions of the song.

Extensions

1. After they finish, ask students to make a list of which words they could easily catch and which they could not. In this way dictation can serve as an indicator of what words and sounds are giving them trouble and gives you an indication of where to work in the future.

2. Work in groups; compete to see who finishes first.

3. For variations look at **More dictation (45)**.

Links

For similar techniques see **Pop songs (32)** or **The cloze passage (23).**

45   More dictation

**Secondary
focus:**   discussion
                 vocabulary
                 singing

Song type: short, slow songs

Level: very low to intermediate

Purpose: facilitating dictation

Students: adults and children

When using dictation, any data you give your students helps them and makes their job easier — the trick is to give enough information while still challenging them. This activity describes several levels of help. Each step gives more help.

1. Give students very little help, only the title of the song and some of the words. List the words on the board in alphabetical order.

2. Give some phrases, especially prepositional phrases.

3. Write a blank outline of the song on the board or hand-out. This tells them the number of words per line. Draw a line for every word. For example, the song *Row, Row, Row Your Boat* would look like this:

    ____ ____ ____ ____ ____
    ____ ____ ____ ____
    ____ ____ ____ ____
    ____ ____ ____ ____ ____

4. Do the same as number 3, but include some of the words.

    Row Row ____ ____ ____
    ____ down the stream
    Merrily ____ ____ ____
    ____ ____ but a ____

Alternative

Give the first two lines. In the following line omit the last word. Continue to omit words. This idea, as well as the song *Footsteps in the Sand*, is from Ken Wilson.

I'm writing you a letter
I write one every day.
I'm looking at . . .
But I don't know . . .
I saw . . .
I . . .
. . . .
. . . . right away
. . . . . . on the phone.

46 Guided story writing

Secondary focus: discussion

Song type: songs that tell stories

Level: low to intermediate

Purpose: encouraging creative writing

Students: adults and children

To encourage creative writing, use a song that tells a story, delete part of the song and ask students to write their own ending.

Preparation

Select a song that tells a story and decide how much to reveal.

In class

Introduce the song. See Appendix: Sample lesson plans and selected songs, pages 163–6 for two possible lesson plans. Or use a song that you have already introduced and worked with, using another technique. In that case you lose the surprise element, but students can still write an alternative ending. Listen to the song to the point you have decided upon, then ask the class to complete the story.

Options

1. If students are hearing the song for the first time and do not know the ending, take a poll on how they think the story will end. You can take a class poll on how many think it will be a happy ending, a sad ending or a surprise ending.

2. After reading and discussing the endings students have written, take a class vote. Which was the most original, most optimistic, pessimistic, etc.?

3. Stipulate the form the writing must take. Students can be asked to write the story in the form of a personal letter to a friend, a business letter, a newspaper article, a police report, a newspaper article, or other form.

4.   Ask students to draw a picture of the song ending and discuss.

Links

Continue working with the song with other techniques such as **Dialogue drama (47)** or **Point of view (59).**

47   Dialogue drama

Secondary focus:	discussion
Song type:	songs that tell stories
Level:	very low to intermediate
Purpose:	writing dialogues or stories
Students:	adults and children

Preparation

Although no special preparation is necessary, this technique works well with a song you have previously introduced. See Appendix: Sample lesson plans and selected songs, pages 163–6 for two possible lesson plans.

In class

Introduce or review the song. Then divide the song into scenes or acts. Assign each scene to a group of students. Ask them to write dialogues based on the action in the scene. You can stop at this point or continue by combining the dialogues into a narrated story.

Extension

Hold a performance. One or more students can read the narration, another group can be the chorus, while others can be the characters in the song who speak and act out the dialogues.

Links

For related techniques see **Guided story writing (46)** or **Split songs (56).**

48 Song posters

**Secondary
focus:**   discussion

Song type: all songs

Level: very low to intermediate

Purpose: display as revision of lyrics

Students: adults and children

Song lyrics can be arranged in various ways on poster board and displayed in the classroom. These posters can be used to introduce songs or serve as a review of the song. Magazine and other types of pictures enhance the visual appeal. Below are several possibilities.

1. Put the lyrics on one side of the poster and pictures which illustrate the meaning of the song on the other.

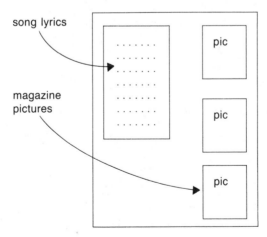

2. Write the lyrics on the poster, but for words that can be drawn or illustrated by small pictures, insert the picture or drawing of the object. If you cannot find pictures, use symbols such as squares and triangles or blocks of colour.

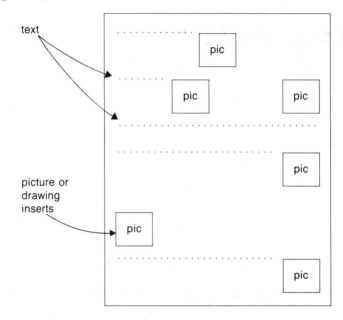

3. Pick a song originally written in another language e.g. *O Christmas Tree*. Put the German words on one side and an English translation on the other.

German	English
. . . .	. . . . . .
. . . .	. . . . . .
. . . .	. . . . . .
. . . .	. . . . . .
. . . .	. . . . . .
. . . .	. . . . . .

4. Cut the lyrics into strips and arrange them in various configurations.

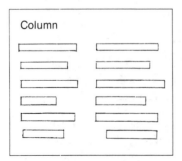
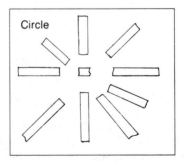

5. Highlight key words or phrases. If you are working with prepositional phrases, for example, underline them or colour them with a highlighter pen.

6. If you cannot display song posters in your room, ask students to make them page size and put them in their notebooks.

Links

For related techniques see **Strip songs (16), Song cards (20), Jumbled words (22)** or **Picture selection (55).**

49 Punctuation

Secondary focus:	listening
Song type:	all songs
Level:	low to intermediate
Purpose:	practising punctuation
Students:	adults and children

This is a good activity to introduce a song. It gives students the lyrics by means of a punctuation task. After you have finished, you can continue with additional activities such as **Vocabulary association (9)** and **Dialogue drama (47)**.

Preparation

Select a song and write out the lyrics with no punctuation.

In class

Introduce this activity by asking students to punctuate a sentence you have written on the board such as: Today, if you want to, we're going to study the song (*name of song*) by (*name of singer*). Pass out the lyrics, listen to the song and ask students to add the punctuation.

Links

For related techniques see **Mistakes (12), Rhythm and stress (33)** and **Breathing easy (36).**

50   Movies in your mind

Secondary focus:	discussion
Song type:	instrumental music
Level:	intermediate
Purpose:	exploiting narrative suggestion by music
Students:	adults

Music has unique powers to excite and influence our imagination. This technique uses instrumental music to allow students access to their internal imagery.

Preparation

Select some instrumental programme music, for example Saint-Saëns, *Carnival of the Animals*; Holst, *The Planets*; Tchaikowsky, *The Nutcracker Suite*.

In class

Tell your students that they will be listening to some music and that you want them to listen with their eyes closed. Tell them to pretend that they are watching a movie, but the movie is in their mind. Listen to the selection for about one minute. Then ask students to write about what they saw in their mind's eye. Students can share their writing in groups or the whole class.

Links

For other techniques using instrumental music see **Theme music (52), Song strings (54), Picture selection (55)** and **Multiple choice (60).**

51 Grammar letter

This exercise uses a song to review a structure by looking at the lyrics as if they were a letter the student had received and inviting the students to write a reply.

Preparation

Prepare the song lyrics by clozing out any points you want reviewed. (For discussion of a cloze, see **The cloze passage — 23**.) In the upper-left-hand corner of the lyric sheet write or type a salutation, 'Dear _____'. At the bottom put in a 'Love' or 'Sincerely Yours'. In this way the song lyrics have become a letter.

In class

Tell your students that today they will study/review the structure(s) you have decided. As an option consider presenting and/or reviewing the letter format. Hand out the clozed form of the song lyrics. Then ask students to write their names after the salutation, Dear _____. Then ask them to write the name of the person who is writing the letter at the bottom of the letter under 'Sincerely Yours'. The letter could, of course, be from anyone, but it is more interesting when the letter is from a famous person everyone in the class knows. If you chose a love song, for example, *True Love*, the person sending the student a letter could be a famous singer, movie star or sports hero. If you chose a holiday song, for example, *Santa Claus is Coming to Town* the person sending the letter could be Father Christmas. Working alone, in pairs or groups, ask the students to fill in the clozed passage before they listen to the song. Then listen to confirm. Ask students individually to write their reply to the sender. It might be helpful to ask students specifically to answer two or three questions. For example, in a letter to Father Christmas students must say whether they have been naughty or nice, give an example and state what present they would like.

Links

For related techniques see **Structure review (21), The cloze passage (23)** or **Punctuation (49).**

52 Theme music

Secondary focus:	grammar discussion
Song type:	instrumental music
Level:	low to intermediate
Purpose:	music suggesting narrative
Students:	adults and children

This technique uses instrumental music to suggest a movie which students describe.

Preparation

Select a piece of instrumental music, especially music that your students might not be familiar with.

In class

Tell them that this music is the theme music of a movie and write questions such as these on the board:

What kind of movie is it? (action, mystery, police, comedy, SF, thriller, adventure, etc.)
Where does the movie take place?
What is the time of the movie, now, ten years ago, etc.?
What is the name of the movie?

Now write the story line of the movie. For example, a policeman looks into a store and sees a hold-up going on and . . .

Links

For related techniques see **Guided story writing (46), Movies in your mind (50)** and **Visualisation (53).**

SECTION 5

DISCUSSION

Introduction

Songs and music contain highly concentrated emotion, imaginative situations and narrative possibilities. A short song can provide many hours' worth of discussion with your students — extrapolating from the situation, considering the themes and issues raised in the song, and using the elements of the song as springboards for their own ideas.

53 Visualisation

Song type: instrumental music

Level: intermediate

Purpose: to elicit description of scenes from music

Students: adults

One of the properties of instrumental music is its ability to produce strong images in the minds of its listeners. These images can be drawn and used as the basis for discussion.

Preparation

Select a piece of instrumental music that does not tell a story. It is a good idea if the students are not familiar with or have strong associations with the music. For example, some movie music is so familiar that if you play it, students will tell you about the movie.

In class

Tell the students to relax, that they are going to listen to some music, but do not tell them the type or name of the music. Play the music. You will have to decide how long, but about one minute should be sufficient. Ask students to close their eyes and relax. Do not discuss the music but ask students to take pen or pencil and paper and draw the picture that was in their mind when they were listening. If a student tells you that he felt warm, happy, sad, etc. this is not what you are after. Images in our minds are very concrete. Students should be able to tell you what they saw as clearly as if they were describing a photograph. The class discussion, in small groups or the class as a whole, can take only a few minutes or take most of the period.

Possible sources of music

Music from parts of the world and cultures the students are not familiar with; consider New Age music or even sounds such as the sound of water, the wind etc.

Links

For other techniques using instrumental music see **BGM (25), Movies in your mind (50), Theme music (52), Song strings (54), Picture selection (55), Multiple choice (60)** and **Sound quiz (74).**

54 Song strings

Secondary focus:	writing
	grammar
Song type:	instrumental music
Level:	low to intermediate
Purpose:	associations and comparisons
Students:	adults and children

Instrumental music can be gathered and used for many purposes. Song strings are short recordings of fifteen to twenty seconds of several pieces of instrumental music. To make a song string, gather several song tapes and record parts of them, thus creating a new tape. You can use this new tape, your song string, for several activities.

Preparation

Decide on the type of song string you want and your teaching point. For example, if your teaching point is the names of countries, music might come from tapes such as the following:

Country	Name of album
India	*The Genius of Ravi Shankar* (CBS PCT 9560)
USA	*Benny Goodman, Let's Dance* (Capitol 4XL-9090)
China	*Chinese Classical Music* (Fung Hang Records CCMC 09)
Japan	*Japanese Folk Melodies* (Jean-Pierre Rampal, CBS MT 35862)
Germany	*Bach's Toccata and Fugue in D minor*

In class

Play the song string and ask for impressions. Can anyone identify any of the music? Play it again and ask students to guess which country each piece of music comes from. If you have a world map in the room, students can locate the country.

114

Then give students some pictures depicting some aspect of each country and ask students to arrange the pictures in the same order they hear the music and then discuss the picture and its relation to the country. Follow-up activities can include a review of names of countries and what people from those countries are called, questions about those countries, e.g. size, location, population.

Extensions

1. Make other types of song strings. Select time periods, e.g. pop music of the 1940s, 1950s, 1960s, 1970s etc., or types of music, e.g. jazz, New Age, rock, soul, country and western; other types of music such as baroque, romantic, electronic, post-romantic; or compare instruments, e.g. the bagpipes, drums, horns.

2. Listen to a song string and ask students to write any associations they have as they listen.

3. Instead of selecting magazine pictures that depict some aspect of the culture, select pictures on another theme. For example, select only pictures of animals. Ask students to select which animals they would pair with each selection on the song string. Other types of pictures might be ordinary people, objects, famous persons, or cities.

4. Instead of giving students one picture for every piece of music on your song string, give them several. Or try giving them pictures which in your opinion have absolutely no connection with any of the music and see what happens.

5. Make a song string entirely of sounds rather than music. See *Sounds Intriguing* or *Sounds Interesting* by Maley and Duff for some recorded sounds or go to a library for sound-effects records. For techniques on using sound see **Sounds nice (72)** or **Sound quiz (74)**.

6. For a lower-level class use song strings to practise expressing likes and dislikes. For a higher class, use song strings to practise the language of comparison and contrast. See **Song competition (68)**.

Links

For other techniques using instrumental music see **BGM (25), Movies in your mind (50), Theme music (52), Visualisation (53), Picture selection (55), Multiple choice (60)** and **Sound quiz (74).**

55 Picture selection

Secondary focus:	listening
Song type:	all songs plus instrumental music
Level:	low to intermediate
Purpose:	relating music to pictures
Students:	adults and children

Music is capable of creating images in our imagination. These images can be focused by using magazine pictures or drawings.

Preparation

Select a song and three or four pictures per student. Select some pictures you feel have a connection to the song and select some others at random.

In class

Ask the students to listen to the song and select a picture according to some criterion such as a picture that shows something mentioned in the song; that shows something that you would do if you were a character in the song; that best describes this song, or that has the feeling or mood of the song.

Extension

After discussing, play the song again while students draw their own pictures of the song.

Links

For related techniques see **Drawing the song (2)** or **Movies in your mind (50).**

56 Split songs

Secondary
focus: writing

Song type: songs that tell stories

Level: intermediate

Purpose: jig-saw listening

Students: adults

Songs that tell stories have a beginning, a middle and an end. This technique separates the song into its beginning, middle and end by recording each part of the song on separate tapes. Students listen to one part and guess the other parts of the song.

Preparation

Collect three tape players and select a song that tells a story. See Appendix: Sample lesson plans and selected songs, pages 163—6 for examples of songs that tell stories as well as sample lesson plans. Record each section of the song on a separate tape. You will need a tape player for each group.

In class

Divide the class into the same number of groups into which you have divided your song (three). Give each group a tape that contains one part of the song — the beginning, middle or end. Give each group a tape player, tell them which part of the song they have, and ask them to find a place where they cannot hear the other group. Then ask each group to listen to the tape and make notes on the part of the song they have. Move around the room checking on the progress of each group. Their assignment is to reconstruct the missing parts of the song. If they have the beginning of the song, ask them to finish the story. If they have the middle, ask them how the story begins and ends. If they have the end of the song, ask them to construct the events which support such an ending. Finally, ask each group of students to report their version of the song. You might find there are three versions of the song or you might find that some groups have similar versions. But each group will be amused at what other groups think happened in their part of the story.

Hints

1. Ask the class to tell their version of the story in reverse order. Group 3 (the group that was given the ending) reports first, then group 2 and group 1. That way the suspense is held longer.

2. If the class is small, you might give the whole class one part of the story and ask them to reconstruct the song from the portion they have. You might or might not tell them which part they have.

Links

For related techniques about reconstructing the story see **Strip songs (16), Tell them a story (17), Jumbled words (22), Guided story writing (46)** or **Dialogue drama (47)**. For techniques that deal with visualising the song see **Jacket covers (70)** and **Video warm up (76).**

57 Discussion questions

Song type: songs that tell stories

Level: low to intermediate

Purpose: open discussion

Students: adults and children

This activity uses four types of questions which are referred to as:

1. objective questions,

2. reflective questions,

3. interpretative questions and

4. final questions.

Each type of question has a different function.

Preparation

Listen to the song yourself until you are familiar enough to ask and answer the four types of questions. All the example questions below are based on the song *Bobby Jean* by Bruce Springsteen.

Objective questions

These are questions with obvious answers, such as questions about the characters in the song, the story line, or questions about the singer, the musical style, the place, the time or the sequence of events. Examples of objective questions would be:

What kind of music is this?
What is the girl's name?
How many times does he sing her name?
Which words does he rhyme?
How old were they when they met?
He says they went walking. What was the weather like?
What is a motel?

Have you ever walked in the rain?
What is the advantage of walking with someone in the rain?
Why does he miss her so much?
Do you ever think about running away?

Reflective questions

These are questions that ask about students' reactions and feelings. Examples would be:

They met when they were sixteen; how old do you think they are now?
Do you think she will ever hear the song?
If so, what do you think she will do?
How do you feel when you listen to this song?

Interpretative questions

These ask about meaning and why the characters acted as they did. Some examples are:

Why do you think she ran away?
What are some reasons people run away?
If you ever ran away, where would you go?

Final questions

These ask about the deepest parts of our lives. Most teachers do not usually ask questions at this level unless they know their students quite well, but these examples are included to indicate what could be done. Teachers asking questions at this level should be comfortable asking and answering these questions themselves before asking others.

Who would you like to walk with in the rain?
Everybody is running from something; what are you running from now?

Hints

1. Ask a lot of objective questions, some reflective questions, one or two interpretative questions and *maybe* one final-level question.

2. It is very important that you ask the objective questions first, the reflective questions next and so on. This sequence is not optional. The human mind needs something objective on which to hang its reflections.

Links

For another type of question, see **All-purpose questions (24).**

58 Feelings

Song type:	all songs
Level:	intermediate
Purpose:	discussing feelings
Students:	adults

All songs express feelings and this activity can be used to identify and discuss feelings or supplement a text lesson on that theme.

Preparation

Select a song, and if you have not introduced it decide how to do that.

In class

Begin with a contextual statement such as: 'Today we are going to study and discuss how the (L-2) language deals with feelings. How are you feeling today?' Review feeling words or use this technique to review a text lesson on feelings, e.g. happy, sad, stressed-out etc. Listen to the song and ask: 'What are the feelings in this song?' List on the board. This chart can be used as a basis for your discussion.

Feeling Word	What causes you to feel this way?	What do you do when you have this feeling?
	I feel _____ when X makes me feel _____	• call my friend • go shopping • eat • take a walk

Possible follow-up discussion questions

Tell me a movie or TV programme where you saw the same feeling as in this song.
    What happened in the scene to make someone feel that way?

What advertisement in a newspaper, magazine, underground or bus illustrates this
feeling or makes suggestions on how to have this feeling?

What are some other songs that have this same feeling?

How do women express this feeling? How do men?

Does our society think this feeling is a good one to have? How does it encourage
or discourage people from having this feeling?

Links

For related techniques on feeling see **Movies in your mind (50)**, **Point of view (59)**,
Multiple choice (60) and **Values (65)**.

59 Point of view

Secondary focus: writing

Song type: songs that tell stories

Level: intermediate

Purpose: clarification

Students: adults

Many songs are about characters whose actions and motivations can be used for discussion exercises. One way to have a class discussion is to fill out the chart provided in this exercise.

Preparation

No special preparation is necessary.

In class

Introduce or review the song. Then draw a grid on the board with one space for every character or group in the song that you want to discuss. In the last space write 'You' for opinions students want to express but which are not those of character 1, etc.

	Character 1	Character 2	You
Question 1: What is the problem for this character?			
Question 2: How does the character deal with the problem?			

Ask students to write what they think is each character's point of view relative to the questions in the grid. Ask the students to consider what the character thinks and why they act as they do. Fill out the grid for a whole class discussion.

Additional discussion questions

1. What is probably going to happen to each character in the future?
2. In real life, do you know of anyone in this situation? What did they do?
3. What would you do if you were in that situation?

Extensions

1. Ask students to work individually to fill out the chart. Then work in pairs to compare answers. Then in groups of fours. Finally have a whole class discussion.

2. Try this with songs that do not tell a story but have more than one view presented in the song.

3. Since you are asking for personal opinions, you cannot disagree. Push for clarification with questions such as, 'Where in the song does it say that?' and 'What makes that a problem?'

4. Distinguish between situations (cannot do anything about it) and problems (can do something). For example, in the song *Rudolph the Red-nosed Reindeer* if the students say the problem for Santa Claus is that the weather is foggy, point out that weather is not a problem because you cannot do anything about it. Ask questions that raise the issue of what Santa can do (secure navigational equipment in the form of Rudolph's nose).

Links

For related techniques see **Split songs (56), Multiple choice (60)** and **Values (65).**

60 Multiple choice

Secondary
focus: listening

Song type: instrumental music

Level: intermediate

Purpose: discussing reactions to music

Students: adults

This is a right-brained multiple-choice activity which asks students to listen to instrumental music and mark a level of response. The response provides the basis for discussion.

Preparation

Prepare one or more short music excerpts (a minute or a minute and a half). See **Song strings (54)** for ideas on types of music. Also decide whether you want to make a hand-out or write the questions below on the board. Change any of the questions below the better to fit your situation.

In class

Listen to the music and check (√) how you feel.

 √ I means a strong yes

 √ II means a weak yes

 √ III means a weak no

 √ IV means a strong no

1. If you turned on the radio and heard this music, would you:

	I	II	III	IV
(a) turn it off immediately?				
(b) listen and try to find out the title?				
(c) buy the record or tape?				
(d) leave it on as background music?				

2. What nationality do you think the composer is?

	I	II	III	IV
(a) Swiss				
(b) English				
(c) Japanese				
(d) German				
(e) American				
(f) Other				

3. When you listen to this music, do you think about:

	I	II	III	IV
(a) love and passion				
(b) war				
(c) a scene in the country				
(d) a season				
(e) water and the sea				
(f) something else				

4. How do you feel when you listen to this music?

	I	II	III	IV
(a) frightened and depressed				
(b) sad				
(c) relaxed				
(d) tense				
(e) other				

Hints

1. Try different types of instrumental music such as classical, New Age, folk dances or songs in languages that the students do not know.

2. Try different questions such as:
    'What room in the house does this music remind you of?'
    'What colour?'
    'What scene?'
    'Which city or country?'

Links

For related activities see **Theme music (52), Visualisation (53), Song strings (54), Where is the music? (61),** and **Musical memories (62)**

61 Where is the music?

<table>
<tr><td>**Secondary focus:**</td><td>writing
listening</td></tr>
<tr><td>**Song type:**</td><td>not applicable</td></tr>
<tr><td>**Level:**</td><td>low to intermediate</td></tr>
<tr><td>**Purpose:**</td><td>sensitivity to environmental music</td></tr>
<tr><td>**Students:**</td><td>adults</td></tr>
</table>

To heighten awareness of their musical environment, this exercise asks students to become aware of what music they hear, where they hear it and what purpose the music seems to be serving.

Preparation

No preparation is necessary.

In class

Ask students to close their eyes and mentally retrace their steps as they left home. Where did they hear music? What kind was it? The board might look like the example below.

Where did you hear music today?	What kind was it?	What was it there for? What purpose was it serving?
radio soundtruck coffee shop inside store street	BGM popular music a jingle	politics relaxation advertising

Then ask students actually to go out and do it. Ask them to walk from place X to place Y. This could be a normal trip they often take, such as from their home to school, or a special walk. Walking places might include a main street and a side street, or across campus and a walk in the country. Ask them to go into such places as shopping centres, hotels, bus stations, train stations. Ask them to take notes and write the data under such headings as day of week, time of day and location. Then report to the class. They could do this survey individually or in groups.

Links

For related techniques see **Music survey (64), Sounds nice (72)** and **Sound quiz (74).**

62   Musical memories

Song type: not applicable

Level: intermediate

Purpose: recalling past music

Students: adults

We all have experiences with music from an early age. This exercise uses memories associated with those early musical experiences as the basis for a discussion.

Preparation

Prepare the list below as a hand-out or write it on the board. Decide if you want to add some additional categories of your own. Finally, reflect on your own musical memories and do the exercise below. Then use your own musical memory to introduce the exercise.

In class

Open this exercise with the observation that most of us have memories of music and then tell one of yours. Give the students the hand-out or write it on the board. Allow enough time for the students to read the questions and ask questions.

I remember . . .	clearly	vaguely	not at all
1. the first time I whistled	_____	_____	_____
2. my first record player	_____	_____	_____
3. my first music teacher	_____	_____	_____
4. the first time I saw a band	_____	_____	_____
5. my favourite record in secondary school	_____	_____	_____
6. my favourite record jacket	_____	_____	_____
7. a song my mother sang	_____	_____	_____
8. my brother/sister's favourite song	_____	_____	_____
9. my first musical instrument	_____	_____	_____
10. the last concert I attended	_____	_____	_____

Ask the students to tick off (√) one of the three categories for all the questions. For class discussion, ask students which questions they want to answer.

Links

For related techniques see **Music survey (64)** and **Songs that say a lot (73).**

63 Clichés, proverbs and sayings

Secondary focus:	writing
Song type:	long songs
Level:	intermediate
Purpose:	focusing on idioms
Students:	adults

Many songs contain clichés, sayings and proverbs which are of interest to language learners and can become the basis for a discussion.

Preparation

You might want to review these common terms with the class, as they tend to come up in the discussion: slang, saying, cliché, idiom and proverb.

Slang is very informal speech that is usually colourful, playful and sometimes vulgar and socially taboo. Some slang is short-lived. It is often difficult to give an exact definition.

A cliché is a common expression that has been used so often that it is not considered original or interesting in writing and should be avoided, but is commonly used in speaking, e.g. 'Have a good day.'

An idiom is an expression whose meaning cannot be guessed or understood by looking at or understanding each individual word, e.g. 'catch a bus'.

A proverb is a short, popular saying that expresses a common truth or useful thought, e.g. 'An apple a day keeps the doctor away.'

A saying is similar to a proverb. It is short and instructive, e.g. 'All that glitters is not gold.'

In class

Introduce the song with one or two appropriate techniques. See **Making connections (29), Pop songs (32), Mistakes (12)** or **Song word puzzles (11)**. Hand out the song lyrics (if you have not already done so) and ask students to underline what they think are slang expressions, clichés, idioms, proverbs or sayings. Also ask them to underline other interesting phrases that they would like to discuss or remember. Then give students the form below.

Name of song _____

A. Write the key expression _____

_____

B. Rewrite the expression in your own words

_____

_____

C. List three types of people you would use this expression with and three types
   of people you would avoid using it with

   would 1. _____   would avoid 1. _____

   2. _____   2. _____

   3. _____   3. _____

D. Work with a partner or group. Make a short dialogue. Make sure you include
   the key expression

E. Do you have this expression in your language? Write it here

_____

_____

Links

For related activities see **Feelings (58), Values (65)** or **Abstract words (69).**

64 Music survey

Secondary focus:	writing
Song type:	not applicable
Level:	low to intermediate
Purpose:	filling in a questionnaire
Students:	adults

Teachers over twenty-five or thirty are a generation removed from their college-age students. Since each generation has its own musical taste, the purpose of this technique is to give the teacher a way to find out what the new generation is listening to or, in the case of older students, to find out what they listened to.

Preparation

Look at the form below and decide if you want to change any questions.

In class

Explain to your students that you are interested in what music they listen to and that you would like them to complete this music survey. Hand out the survey. Collect individual surveys or tabulate the results on a master form.

Music survey

First name _____   Last name _____
Date   _____   Class _____
Sex _____   Age _____   Country _____

What kind of music do you like? Rate first with 1, second with 2, etc.
Pop _____ Rock _____ Country _____ Jazz _____ Disco _____
Classical _____ Easy listening _____ Folk _____ Other _____

What radio station do you listen to most? _____

Do you listen to music videos on TV? Yes No What is the name of the
programme? _____ What channel? _____

Where do you usually listen to music? Check 1, 2, 3, etc.
your room _____ coffee shop _____ car _____ friend's house _____
on bus, train, bicycle (walkman) _____ restaurant _____ other _____

List three favourite singers or groups
[1] _____
[2] _____
[3] _____

What are your three favourite songs?
[1] _____
[2] _____
[3] _____

How much (%) do you listen to music in English _____ Other _____

Extensions

1. Ask additional questions:
    Do you sing in the bathtub, shower?
    Do you go to sleep with music?
    Do you wake up to music?
    Do you play an instrument?
    Do you sing with a group?

2. Ask students to make up their own questions.

3. The survey can be done in class or students can take it out in the community.

4. Make a class hit parade by listing the top forty songs the class likes.

5. Ask class to write an article for the school newspaper.

Links

For related techniques see **Musical memories (62)** and **Tell me a song about . . . (67).**

65 Values

Song type: long songs

Level: intermediate

Purpose: exploring cultural values

Students: adults

Song lyrics reflect social values. It is helpful and interesting for students learning the language of another culture to become aware of, examine and clarify these values as a way of examining and clarifying their own values.

Preparation

Select a song. This technique is a good follow-up exercise for a song you have previously worked with.

In class

Ask your students to say or write in their own words the main idea of the song. See the chart below. Tell them that this is to be their opinion and there is no correct answer, but that it has to make sense. The purpose of this step is to get a quick overview of the song and set the context for the discussion, so do not spend much time discussing this point. Next ask what a value is. Ask them to tell you some other words that mean the same thing as a value. List the words or phrases and do not discuss them in detail. The purpose of this step is to establish criteria for later discussion.

Now ask the students to list some key words in the song that state the main idea of the song. The purpose of this question is to get the students to look carefully at the lyrics. Do not get into a long discussion about why they selected the words they did. These words or phrases will be your springboard into the main discussion. Get several on the board so that you have several entries into the discussion. Select one of the words and ask the class what is the value? Write it in the space provided in the board chart. Often students give a description of the action in the song rather than the statement of a value. If you do receive a description of an action in the song, e.g. she wrote a letter, ask how is this a value or what is the value in writing a letter? Refer to their descriptions of a value. This discussion and clarification is the payoff.

Board

Write the theme or main idea here		
What is a value?	What are some words in the song that state a key idea or theme?	Values in this song
1. . . . . 2. . . . . 3. . . . . 4. . . . . 5. . . . . 6.		1. . . . . 2. . . . . 3. . . . .

Possible follow-up questions

1. What type of people believe in this value?

2. Why do people hold this value? What good is it?

3. I agree (or disagree) with this value. What do you think?

4. Do you think this value is universal? (or Canadian, American, Australian, British, the students' country, etc.)

Links

For related techniques see **Point of view (59), Multiple choice (60)** or **Cultural stereotypes (75).**

66 Theme words

Secondary focus: listening

Song type: all songs

Level: low to intermediate

Purpose: identifying themes

Students: adults

Many songs have a fairly obvious theme. This technique allows you to use a song's theme for class discussion.

Preparation

Select a song that has a theme you want to discuss. Then think of idiomatic phrases, sayings, proverbs, etc. that illustrate the theme and write them on cards. For example, in the song *Isn't It Nice to be Home Again* by James Taylor, the theme is home. There are many possible phrases: home sweet home, homesick, home is where the heart is, there's no place like home, make yourself at home, and home away from home.

In class

Hand out the cards. Ask students to work in pairs or groups to decide what they think the phrase means. Ask students to come up with a situation in which they could use the phrase and write a dialogue that clearly shows the meaning. Finally, focus on one phrase. Ask students to draw or write something that illustrates the phrase. For example, if you used the phrase 'home away from home' students would draw or write a favourite place. Put all the pieces of paper in a box. Pick out the drawings one by one and guess whose it is and why.

Links

For related techniques see **Drawing the song (2), Song poetry (15)** and **Theme music (52).**

67 Tell me a song about . . .

Song type: not applicable

Level: low to intermediate

Purpose: remembering song titles

Students: adults

Many foreign-language students have been exposed to a wide variety of English-language songs. While they may or may not have memorised the complete lyrics, frequently they can remember the song title and what the song is about. This technique asks students to use their cultural memory and match song themes with song titles.

Preparation

Decide how to configure the class, e.g. work individually, pairs or small groups.

In class

Give the students a theme such as love, friendship, time, places, travel, men, women, colour, cars, weather, drinking, Christmas etc. Then ask them to tell you three song titles on the theme. Use this technique to get students talking or as a way of introducing a type of song or a discussion theme.

   To make this activity into a game, give one point for each correct answer. Or ask all students to stand up. When a student gives a correct answer, he or she can sit down.

Links

For related techniques see **Music survey (64)** and **Trivia (71).**

68 Song competition

Secondary focus: writing

Song type: all songs

Level: very low to intermediate

Purpose: comparing songs

Students: adults and children

This activity asks students to compare songs and indicate which one or ones they liked and why. It has variations rather than steps.

Variation 1

Compare *one* song sung by more than one singer or group. You must have two or three recordings of the same song, each by a different artist, for example *September Song* as sung by Willie Nelson, the Platters or Lou Reed. In addition to finding more than one recording, you must also decide the voting procedure to choose which recording students prefer and why. One way is to ask students to rank all the songs in the order of preference. Another is to ask students to select one favourite only and a third way is to assign a points system, e.g. three points to first choice, two points to second choice and so on. You can stipulate selection criteria such as voice, rhythm, style, instrumentation, etc.

Variation 2

Select *two or more* different songs all sung by the same artist and follow the same procedures above.

Variation 3

Compare *two or more* songs according to some criterion. This grid is from *The Cambridge English Course* by Michael Swan and Catherine Walter, Book 2, Cambridge: Cambridge University Press, 1985.

	tune	words	singer
Song number 1	√		
Song number 2		X	
Song number 3			=

√ means like, X means do not like, = means no opinion

Hints

1. There is no reason to stick with popular songs only. Try chamber music, opera or symphonies. Or compare different types of music, for example classical and rock.

2. If you have a multi-cultural classroom, ask students to bring in music from their cultures and discuss. To see how this can be turned into an academic writing project, read the excellent article by Jill Van Cleve (see Reference, page 159).

3. Compare national anthems from various countries. What are the concepts? values? historical background? who wrote them? when?

4. Compare songs that state different views of the same subject, e.g. on the subject of money, compare the song *Easy Street* which disdains money and *Money Changes Everything* which glorifies it.

Links

For related techniques see **Two versions (34)** and **Song strings (54).**

69 Abstract words

Secondary focus:	vocabulary
Song type:	all songs
Level:	low to intermediate
Purpose:	discussing song vocabulary
Students:	adults

Some songs use concrete words to tell their story or express their feelings, while other songs use vague and abstract words. This technique deals with vague and abstract words and makes them concrete by making them personal.

Preparation

Select a song and make a list of the vague or abstract words.

In class

Introduce or review the song. Then give the list of abstract words to your students. Answer any questions students may have and then ask students to work individually and rank the words according to a criterion you give them, e.g.

1. most important qualities in yourself,

2. most important in a marriage partner or friend,

3. friendly (or unfriendly) words.

Then ask the students to work in groups. Tell them that they must arrive at a group consensus and that they will have to discuss until they can agree. If desired, groups can report to the larger class.

Links

For related techniques that sensitise students to words see **Definitions (14), The cloze passage (23), Paraphrasing (43), Feelings (58)** and **Clichés, proverbs and sayings (63).**

70   Jacket covers

Secondary focus: writing

Song type: not applicable

Level: intermediate

Purpose: relating pictures to songs

Students: adults

Record, cassette and CD jacket covers are designed to catch our attention, advertise their contents and entice us to buy. To do this they must reflect current cultural values and incorporate modern graphic design. This technique asks students to look at record covers closely, to examine the cultural values and to design a cover themselves.

Preparation

Gather some jacket covers. Also some magazine pictures, cardboard and pens.

In class

Pass out the record jackets. Ask the students to select one, examine it carefully and list on the board the type of information they find, e.g. name of the album, recording date, historical background, pictures, etc. Then invite students to look at all the covers. If there is one artist or group with several jackets that represent recordings over a period of time, compare the oldest cover with the newest cover. Ask students what differences and changes they notice. Are they able to say what values are being presented in record jackets of the 1960s, 1970s, 1980s, 1990s.

As a class project, ask students to design their own jacket cover. Divide into groups and ask each group to decide what kind of music, e.g. jazz, country, rock? What is the name of their group? What pictures and information do they want on their cover? What are the names of the songs? Tell your students to use cardboard, magazine pictures or even photographs to design and create their own cover.

Links

For related techniques see **Song posters (48)** and **Picture selection (55).**

71 Trivia

This is a quiz game in which trivia questions about music, singers and groups are asked in class during a designated discussion time. The purpose of this game is:

1. to give cultural background of music, singers and groups;

2. to check listening — how well your students pay attention to what you and others in the class say; and

3. to review past time and prepositions of time.

   The trivia quiz requires three steps:

   (a) first, you must provide material for the quiz,

   (b) next, engage in class discussions,

   (c) and finally, hold the trivia quiz.

Preparation

Keep a piece of paper or some cards handy for taking notes.

In class

One way to provide material for the quiz is by taking notes on any discussion you or your students have in which an interesting fact about music arises. For example, which groups are in town, who is popular now, who has a new song or album out, which groups have broken up. These notes can be the basis for your quiz questions.

Engage in class discussions by scheduling a music gossip session in your class on a regular basis, e.g. the first ten minutes of class. It will give you an opportunity to teach vocabulary items such as 'gossip' and 'have you heard?' To ensure that such discussions occur, take steps such as the following:

1. Bring in fan magazines and discuss an article.

2. Check your local newspaper for music news, for example concert listings. Discuss these articles in class; include classical music as well as rock and pop groups.

3. Ask questions about where people can go to hear free concerts in your city, the best jazz spots, which local musicians are playing and where.

4. To make the trivia quiz into a listening exercise, bring in short tapes of announcements you have recorded from radio or TV. This brings another voice into the classroom and provides another source of trivia questions. If you teach where there is no radio or TV in English, then tape another teacher reading announcements or short articles.

Finally, hold a trivia quiz. Use the questions you have written on your cards. The quiz can be a short review or it can be the main activity for the period.

Extensions

1. Working with the class as a whole or in groups, ask students to make up their own questions. After students have written their questions and you have corrected them, ask the students to read them.

2. Adapt this format to other areas of student interest; for example, fashion news, sports news or business news.

Links

For related techniques see **Where is the music? (61)** and **Video warm up (76).**

72 Sounds nice

Secondary focus: writing

Song type: not applicable

Level: low to intermediate

Purpose: sensitivity to environmental sounds

Students: adults

Identifying and becoming more aware of the sounds students hear in their daily life may increase awareness, generate classroom conversation and help improve sound environments in the future.

Preparation

No special preparation is necessary.

In class

Ask students to work individually and list the five sounds they like the best and the five sounds they dislike the most. Read and discuss the sounds. If possible, ask the students to go outside and take a walk, being careful not to talk to each other or even walk together, as the sound of their footsteps might muffle sounds they might otherwise hear. Then repeat step one with reference to the sounds they heard outside. This might be a good follow-up after **Sound quiz (74)**.

Links

For related exercises see **Where is the music? (61)** and **Sound quiz (74).**

73   Songs that say a lot

Secondary focus: writing

Song type: not applicable

Level: low to intermediate

Purpose: recalling significant songs

Students: adults

By recalling songs and music from our past we can enjoy, enrich and share the memories.

Preparation

No special preparation is necessary.

In class

Ask students to think back to their childhood or early school years and remember songs or melodies. Some categories are:

> songs your mother sang to you
> songs your brothers and sisters liked
> early school songs
> secondary school and junior school songs
> songs that were popular while you were in junior or senior school
> songs popular while you were in university
> songs that have a special meaning and memory for you

Ask students to write what they can remember, e.g. a title, some words or a phrase. Ask students if they can hum or sing a little of the song. Some students may have tapes or records they can bring to class.

Ask students to discuss (or write about) questions such as:

Where were you when you heard this song or music?

How old were you?
What memories do you have?

Links

For related techniques see **Musical memories (62)**, **Music survey (64)** and **Tell me a song about ... (67).**

74 Sound quiz

Song type: not applicable

Level: low to intermediate

Purpose: introducing sound words

Students: adults

There has always been a close relationship between everyday sounds and music and, according to Murray Schafer, 'this blurring of the edges between music and environmental sounds may eventually prove to be the most striking feature of all twentieth-century music'.

Preparation

List some sounds with which students are likely to be familiar, including some sounds you think they will like and some you think they will not like.

In class

As a warm up, ask students to sit quietly, close their eyes and listen. See how many sounds you and the class can identify. Then hand out your sound list. Which sound do you like the best? Mark that sound with 1. Then mark the next sound you like with 2 and so on until you have ranked all the sounds from 1 to 15.

_____ a woman's high heels clicking
_____ train platform announcement
_____ wood crackling as it burns
_____ person walking in slippers
_____ dog barking
_____ book closing
_____ cat purring
_____ a filing cabinet closing
_____ camera shutter clicking
_____ person blowing his/her nose
_____ thunder clapping

_____ water gurgling
_____ railway crossing bells clanging
_____ siren wailing
_____ rain pattering on the roof

Go over the list for meaning. Ask students to evaluate the sounds by ranking them by preference 1, 2, 3 etc. Continue working with the list of sounds by asking students to divide the list according to one of the categories below:

(a) sounds they hear inside the house and sounds they hear outside;
(b) sounds they hear every day and sounds they seldom hear;
(c) night sounds and day sounds;
(d) sounds of the city and sounds of the country;
(e) sounds that remind them of school and sounds that remind them of home.

Finally, working individually or in groups, ask students to look at the sound list, select one sound and then write or say something about that sound such as:

Where do you usually hear this sound?
What time do you hear it? day or night?
Who or what makes the sound?
What are they doing?
What is an experience you have had involving this sound?

Extensions

1. Take some objects such as keys, coins, cassette case, scissors, pencil and chalk to class to make some sounds. With these objects and objects usually found in any classroom you can make the following sounds:

    (a) keys dropping on table (or jingling coins)
    (b) knocking on door or table
    (c) cutting paper with scissors (or tearing paper)
    (d) scraping chair on floor
    (e) tapping cassette case with pencil
    (f) rapping window (or wall)
    (g) snapping fingers (or clapping)
    (h) coughing (or sighing)
    (i) writing on board with chalk
    (j) whistling (or humming)

    Ask the students to close their eyes and guess what the sounds are. Substitute these sounds for the sound worksheet.

2. Make your own tape of sounds. Between ten and fifteen sounds should be adequate. If you have a tape recorder with a mike, you can make your own recording of

sounds in your home, school or community; this could also be a class project. You can also use a sound-effects record or Maley and Duff's *Sounds Interesting* or *Sounds Intriguing*. Make a worksheet and ask students to draw a line to what they think the sound is.

Sequence on tape sounds

(a) description of sound A
(b) description of sound B
(c) and so on

Substitute these sounds for the sound worksheet.

Links

For related techniques see **Where is the music? (61)** and **Sounds nice (72).**

Following are some additional examples of sounds:

church or temple bells ringing	window opening or closing
clock ticking	footsteps shuffling in the hall
train whistle blowing	footsteps grinding on sand or gravel
jet aircraft engine whining	electric motor humming
propeller aircraft	frogs croaking
opening or closing a desk drawer	dishes clattering in restaurant
birds singing, chirping	person grunting or groaning
hammering	telephone ringing
coins jingling	book closing with a thud
crowd cheering	sewing machine clicking
radio blaring	tradesmen's songs
toilet flushing	cat purring
marching band playing	cicadas singing
voices whispering	crickets chirping
singing	surf pounding on the beach
people laughing	scraping of chairs
a person coughing	typewriter clacking
bees, flies, mosquitoes buzzing	airport flight announcements
children yelling	water cascading
car horns blaring	waves lapping on a beach
tea kettle singing	wind whispering in trees
snake hissing	computer printer
person breathing	water in fountain
small bells tinkling	heart beating
computer printer	a person sniffling

75 Cultural stereotypes

Secondary focus: writing
vocabulary

Song type: all songs

Level: low to intermediate

Purpose: discussing stereotypes

Students: adults

Every country, culture and region of the world has certain stereotypes which are often celebrated in song. For example, one of the stereotypes of Americans is the cowboy. This technique can be used to introduce a song, expand vocabulary and examine students' attitudes towards other people.

Preparation

Select a song that contains a stereotypical image and gather some pictures that illustrate the stereotype.

In class

Listen to the song and discuss what makes this song British, Australian, American, etc. Now pass out the pictures showing some typical scenes of the stereotype in the song. For example, if the song is about a cowboy, pictures could show cowboys, horses, saddles, cows, etc. Ask students to make a list of the items they see in the pictures. Listen to the song and note which items on their list they heard in the song. Hand out the lyrics to verify. Write the word 'stereotype' on the board and discuss. Give students some examples of stereotypes. For Americans, a stereotype might be that all Spanish women dance the flamenco. Ask students to write statements about the culture of the language you are teaching. For example, complete a sentence such as, 'Irish people all _____' or 'A typical French person _____.'

Extensions

1. Hand out or draw a chart on the board that asks students to say what the stereotypes for several types of people are.

Group	Stereotype
Country A, B, etc	
teenagers	
movie stars	
older people	
etc.	

2. Pass out and discuss political cartoons, especially those representing countries, for example, Uncle Sam, John Bull, the Russian bear.

3. Continue the discussion using **Point of view (59)**.

Links

For related techniques see **Vocabulary prediction (1), Song poetry (15), Movies in your mind (50)** or **Values (65)**.

76   Video warm up

Song type: all songs

Level: intermediate

Purpose: comparing song and video

Students: adults

This technique uses music videos as a class warm up activity and need only last from ten to fifteen minutes.

Preparation

Select a music video, set up the video equipment and prepare the song lyrics to be handed out.

In class

Hand out the lyrics to the students to read before watching the video. Explain and discuss any vocabulary questions. Working alone, in pairs or in groups, ask for student impressions of the lyrics, e.g. romantic, depressing, exciting, etc. Then look at the video and compare student first impressions with their impressions after listening. Students are often surprised how their initial response differs after viewing the video.

Extension

Before viewing the song video, look at the song lyrics and ask students to describe how they would direct their own video. Then look at the music video to compare their ideas with what the professional director actually did.

Links

For related techniques see **Picture selection (55)** and **Feelings (58).**

REFERENCES
AND
BIBLIOGRAPHY

References

Abrate, Jayne Halsne (1983) 'Pedagogical applications of the French popular song in the foreign language classroom', *Modern Language Journal* **67** (Spring), 8—12.

Baddock, Barry (1985) 'A musical approach to free language use', *English Teaching Forum* **XXIII**:3 (July), 41.

Bamford, Julian (1982) 'Songs for the teaching', *JALT Newsletter* **VI**:5 (May), 1—3.

Bamford, Julian (1988) 'Music videos and popular music', *The Language Teacher* **XII**:2 (February), 18.

Bartle, G. (1962) 'Music in the language classroom', *The Canadian Modern Language Review* **19**:1 (April), 11—14.

Barzilai, Moshe (1979) 'Using songs creatively', *English Teaching Forum* **XVII**:2 (April), 55.

Booth, Mark W. (1976) 'The art of words in songs', *Quarterly Journal of Speech* **62** (October), 242—9.

Brown, James W. (1975) 'For a pedagogy of the song-poem', *The French Review* **XLIX**:1 (October), 23—31.

Brown, Steve and Marc Helgesen (1988) 'Integrating and extending songs and stories', *Practical English Teaching* (December), 24—5.

Brown, Steve and Marc Helgesen (1989) 'Integrating and extending songs and stories 2', *Practical English Teaching* (March), 19—20.

Campbell, Don G. (1983) *Introduction to the Musical Brain*, St Louis, MO: Magnamusic-Baton, Inc.

Carney, Peter M. (1977) 'Using music to teach English as a second language: A guide to the use of song lyrics', MA thesis, School for International Training, Brattleboro, VT.

Cullen, Louise (1980) 'A new music education for our Canadian multicultural society', *TESL Talk* **II**:1 (Winter), 3—7.

Dickinson, Gillian (1978) 'Using English-teaching songs', in *Selections from MET*, ed. Helen Moorwood, 28, London: Longman Handbooks for Language Teachers.

Dissosway, Patricia (1986) 'Songs in non-aural/oral settings', *The Language Teacher* **X**:10 (September), 19—22.

Donahoe, Betty (1983) 'Review of *Making English Lessons Come Alive*, by Miho Steinberg'. In *JALT Newsletter* **V**:7 (February), 17—19.

Gaunt, Jayne E. (1985) 'The use of popular songs in the ESL classroom', MA thesis, University of Kansas.

Gaunt, Jayne E. (1989) 'The use of popular songs in the writing class', *The Language Teacher* **XIII**:5 (May), 11—13.

Gelman, Manuel (1973) 'Poetry and songs in the teaching of languages', *Babel* **9**:1 (April), 13—15.

Gordon, J.W. (1987) 'Sequenced songplans for the ESL classroom', MA thesis, School for International Training, Brattleboro, VT.

Griffee, Dale T. (1985) 'Accuracy and fluency: Going around in circles', *The Language Teacher* **IX**:2 (February), 21.

Griffee, Dale T. (1986) 'Song Activities', *The Language Teacher* **X**:10 (September), 18—19.

Griffee, Dale T. (1986) 'TESOL songbooks: An annotated bibliography', *The Language Teacher* **X**:10 (September), 23—6.

Griffee, Dale T. (1988) 'Song and music techniques in foreign and second language classrooms', *Cross Currents* **XV**:1 (Fall/Winter), 23—35.

Griffee, Dale T. (1989a) 'Teaching popular songs: Using song types to get started', *The Language Teacher* **XIII**:5 (May), 7—11.

Griffee, Dale T. (1989b) 'An inquiry into the advantages and disadvantages of using songs and music in the language classroom', MA thesis, School for International Training, Brattleboro, VT.

Jolly, Yukiko S. (1975) 'The use of songs in teaching foreign languages', *Modern Language Journal* **59**:1, 11—14.

Katsh, Shelly and Carol Merle-Fishman (1985) *The Music within You*, New York: Simon and Schuster.

Kerr, James Y.K. (1978) 'Musical dictation', in *Selections from MET*, ed. Helen Moorwood, London: Longman Handbooks for Language Teachers.

Kingsbury, Roy and Patrick O'Shea (1979) 'EFL songs for adult elementary learners', *EFL Bulletin* **2**, 5—6, Oxford: Oxford University Press.

Lander, Steve (1988) 'Things to do with songs in the EFL classroom', *English Teachers Association of Switzerland (ETAS) Newsletter* **5**:3 (Summer).

Leith, William D. (1979) 'Advanced French conversation through popular music', *The French Review* **LII**:4 (March), 537—51.

Loew, Helene Z. (1979) 'Tuning in: Popular culture in the second language classroom', *Foreign Language Annals* **12** (December), 271—4.

Maley, Alan (1987) 'Poetry and song as effective language learning activities', in *Interactive Language Teaching*, ed. Wilga Rivers, Cambridge: Cambridge University Press.

Maley, Alan and Alan Duff (1975) *Sounds Interesting*, Cambridge: Cambridge University Press.

Maley, Alan and Alan Duff (1979) *Sounds Intriguing*, Cambridge: Cambridge University Press.

Matthews, Patricia C. (1984) 'Presenting a song — An instant lesson plan', *World Language English* **4**:1 (October), 129—32.

Melpignano, Richard J. (1980) 'A different use for French songs in the classroom', *Foreign Language Annals* **6** (December), 455—7.

Montague, Ashley (1978) *Touching,* 2nd edn, New York: Harper and Row.

Morgan, John and Mario Rinvolucri (1983) *Once Upon a Time*, Cambridge: Cambridge University Press.

Moskowitz, Gertrude (1978) *Caring and Sharing in the Foreign Language Class*, Rowley, MA: Newbury House Publishers.

Munoz, Olivia (1969) 'Focus reports on the teaching of foreign languages number 12', *Songs in the Foreign Language Classroom*, ERICnumber: ED 034450.

Murphy, Tim (1985) 'Teaching for peak relevance using international pop music', *TESOL Newsletter* **XIX**:6 (December), 13.

Ostojic, Branko (1987) 'Music can help', *English Teaching Forum* **XXV**:3 (July), 50—1.

Parker, Sandra L. (1969) 'Using music to teach a second language', *Modern Language Journal* **53**:2, 95—6.

Richards, Regina G. (1975) 'Singing: A fun route to a second language', *The Reading Teacher* (December), 283—5.

Schafer, R. Murray (1980) *The Tuning of the World: Towards a theory of soundscape design*, Philadelphia, PA: University of Pennsylvania Press.

Sommers, Julia Ann (1981) 'Teaching ESL through American songs: A sourcebook', MA thesis, School for International Training, Brattleboro, VT.

Techmeier, Mary (1969) 'Music in the teaching of French', *Modern Language Journal* **53**:2, 96.

Tsai, Shirley Shih-shiang (1982) 'Songs in the ESL classroom — What else beyond pleasure?', MA thesis, School for International Training, Brattleboro, VT.

Vahed, Zubeda (1982) 'Music? I can't play a note!' *TESOL Talk* **13**:3 (Summer), 137−40.

Van Cleve, Jill (1984) 'Using native pop music to enhance the writing process', *TESOL Newsletter* **XVIII**:4 (August), 5.

Vaney, Marianne (1988) 'What can you do with music in a foreign language class', *English Teachers Association of Switzerland Newsletter* **5**, 3.

Wilson, Ken (1985) 'More ideas with songs', *Practical English Teaching* (September), 23−4.

Zola, Meguido and Joachim Sandvoss (1976) 'Song in second-language teaching: The uses of imagery', *Canadian Modern Language Review* **33**:1 (October), 73−85.

Annotated bibliography of ESL/EFL songbooks

ESL songbooks are collections of songs written specially for teaching English as a second or foreign language. Songs in these collections are usually short, and there are about ten to twelve songs in each songbook. They usually come with a record or cassette tape. The quality of the recording varies from poor to excellent. Many of the songbooks reflect the type of songs and musical styles that were popular when they were written and most of the songs were written to illustrate grammatical structures.

Many teachers are unaware of the full range of commercially available ESL songbooks and for that reason I have included a list of some of the songbooks that I am personally familiar with and have used. If you know of a songbook that could be included, please write to me. Be sure to include the title, the publisher, the date and a brief description of the song collection such as the ones that follow.

There is no reason why ESL/EFL songbooks cannot be used in today's communicative classroom. Like popular songs, some ESL songs are better than others. In fact, the best of them could well have appeared on commercial, popular albums. The main problem with ESL songbooks is not quality, but their lack of activities, a problem this book attempts to solve.

The songbooks below are not evaluated; rather, they are listed according to categories. Each is briefly described so you can obtain an idea of the material and can decide whether or not to examine them more closely.

Low-level ESL songbooks

Graham, Carolyn, *The Carolyn Graham Turn of the Century Songbook*, Englewood Cliffs, NJ: Regents, 1982, 96 pp. Student text only. Twenty songs with tape. Graham has written new words to traditional melodies. For example, a song about a red umbrella uses the melody from *Auld Lang Syne*. The tape features Graham, a back-up quartet and a dixieland jazz band. The tape is very helpful, but after hearing it once, almost anyone can sing these traditional melodies. All the songs are simple, frequently having only one verse. In addition, there are large pictures of life in America from the period around 1900 as well as drawings by Charles Dana Gibson. In the back of the text are structurally oriented dialogues and exercises.

Grenough, Millie, *English: Sing it!* New York: McGraw-Hill, 1976, 56 pp. Student text only. Thirty-nine songs with two tapes. Grenough has collected a great variety of songs, from the ABC song to the Beatles. The tape has a clear but antiseptic sound. Some of the songs appear to have been simplified. The strong point of this collection is variety and the large drawings that illustrate the lyrics. There are no drills or exercises. This songbook would be appropriate from children to secondary-school level.

Kind, Uwe, *Tune in to English: Learning English through familiar melodies*, Englewood Cliffs, NJ: Regents, 1980, 108 pp. The text has twenty songs and comes with two tapes. The author uses traditional folk songs from around the world with new lyrics, which are very clever and witty. Each song has a context to explain the situation and this context is recorded. The song collection is intended as a course text and comes with exercises as well as games. Answers are in the back of the book. The table of contents lists the songs and also the functions and structures.

Children's songs

Abe, Keiko and Mary Marquardt (eds), *Let's Sing Together*, Kyobundoh, 1982, 68 pp. This is a collection of American songs, some of which have been simplified for easier understanding. There are thirty-two songs. One page gives the music and words while the facing page contains a drawing which illustrates the song. Many of the songs can be done with actions. There are two tapes. For each song the tape first reads the song and then sings it.

Byrne, John and Anne Waugh (eds), *Jingle Bells and Other Songs*, Oxford, 1982, unnumbered 23 pp. There are twenty-three songs, no teacher book and no tape. This is a collection of American and British songs which have stood the test of time, e.g. *This Old Man, If You're Happy*, and *I Love Sixpence*. Many pictures in colour.

Dakin, Julian (ed.), *Songs and Rhymes*, Harlow: Longman, 1968, reprinted 1978, 42 pp. There are 135 songs and rhymes in this traditional collection. The text is unnumbered. There is a teacher's book which gives some instructions on presentation. There is one tape. Side A has twelve rhymes and eight songs. Side B has twenty-one songs. The text has many small pictures, all in black and white.

Intermediate ESL songbooks

Abbs, Brian and Nola York, *Skyhigh*, Harlow: Longman, 1975. There is a song sheet but no text or teacher book. This collection was intended to be used with the Strategy series. There are thirteen songs on the tape of a pop variety. They are both clear and musical and can be used for listening exercises.

Abbs, Brian and Trevor Jones, *Cloudsongs*, Harlow: Longman, 1977. Eleven songs on one tape, no text or teacher book. These songs are in the mainstream of the pop tradition.

Jones, Christopher, *Back Home*, Harlow: Longman, 1983, 32 pp. Contains twelve songs. The book is large and attractive, with drawings. There are exercises for each song. The song lyrics tend towards subjects that might interest students entering adulthood, e.g. pet cats and job interviewing.

Kingsbury, Roy and Patrick O'Shea, *Sunday Afternoons*, Harlow: Longman, 1974, 55 pp. Student book and teacher book with teaching tips. The tape has all ten songs on one side.

Kingsbury, Roy and Patrick O'Shea, *Seasons and People*, Oxford, 1979, 31 pp. My personal favourite although it is now out of print. If you can find a copy, the song *Summer is Here* is as fresh now as it was then. Twelve songs in a songbook. This collection is strong on singable melodies with several types of music such as Latin, folk, swing and reggae.

Wellman, Laurie and Donald R.H. Byrd, *Hard to Learn that English as a Second Language Blues*, New York: Collier Macmillan, 1975. There are ten songs on the tape; no text or teacher book, but there is a song sheet available. The songs are grammar-oriented as are most of the ESL songs of the 1970s and are performed by a group known as the Brain Trust, who give a clear and professional performance.

Wellman, Laurie and Donald R.H. Byrd, *ESL Express: Easy songs for learning English*, New York: Collier Macmillan, 1976. No text and no teacher book although a song sheet is available. This is an American collection. David Greenberg and Laura Rita Hull give solid performances as the lead singers of the Brain Trust.

Wilson, Ken, *Mister Monday and Other Songs for the Teaching of English*, Harlow: Longman, 1972, (12th impression 1980), 40 pp. Ten songs with a tape and teacher book. The songs were written to illustrate structures, but the Solid British Hat Band gives a professional performance. Though dated, oldie but goodie radio programmes give these songs a familiar ring.

Wilson, Ken and Keith Morrow, *Goodbye Rainbow*, Harlow: Longman, 1975, 56 pp. Twelve songs with the usual structure orientation. Most of the songs retain the folk and protest feeling of the period, but the title song *Goodbye Rainbow* has a timeless quality and *Glitter Hair-Cream* has the charm of an old-fashioned radio commercial.

Traditional songs

Osman, Alice and Jean McConochie (eds), *If You Feel Like Singing*, Harlow: Longman, 1979. Twenty-eight traditional American folk songs. Each song has a picture or drawing illustration, a short reading and three teaching activities. The tape is clear, but recorded by teachers, not professional musicians.

Papa, Mario and Giuliano Iantorno (eds), *Famous British and American Songs and Their Cultural Background*, Harlow: Longman, 1979, 73 pp. No teacher's book. There are thirty-two songs grouped according to categories such as Irish songs, children's songs, sea shanties, drinking songs, Scottish songs, American songs, jazz and Christmas songs. The song is on the left page of the book with a picture and sometimes extensive notes on the right page. The tape is clear and well done.

Songs Alive: English through traditional songs, London: BBC, 1977, reprinted 1978, 56 pp. Eleven songs, all of which tell a story. No teacher book. The tape features high-quality performances by the group Duty Free. The text, which is large with drawings and full-page photos, is part of the BBC's series of ten fifteen-minute video programmes.

Oldies but goodies

Merdinger, Polly and Joel Rosenfeld (eds), *Even If You Can't Carry a Tune . . .*, New York: Newbury House, 1984. Ten old standards, such as *The Tennessee Waltz* and *Under the Boardwalk*, are included. The text also contains grammar, functions, writing and conversation exercises as well as vocabulary. Each lesson has eight pages and the book is designed as a course text.

Appendix: Sample lesson plans and selected songs

This appendix gives groups of activities combined into possible lesson plans. These lesson plans are only a few of the possibilities, but can serve as a way to get started. In addition, you will find a list of selected songs for short, slow songs; songs that tell stories; and short, fast songs.

How many activities are appropriate for one song?

One activity
One song

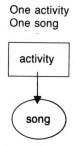

Using one activity for one song may be satisfactory if you have a narrow teaching focus. If you want to concentrate on vocabulary or a particular grammar point, one activity that accomplishes that task may be all you need. It is difficult, however, to move directly to discussion techniques if the class has not worked on the lyrics (vocabulary).

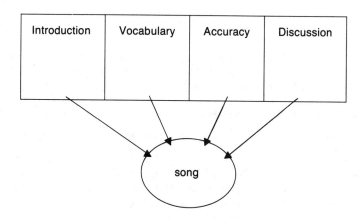

For a more complete lesson plan, several song activities might be desirable. For example, one activity to introduce the song, another activity to deal with vocabulary or lyrics, a third activity for accuracy work and a final activity for class discussion.

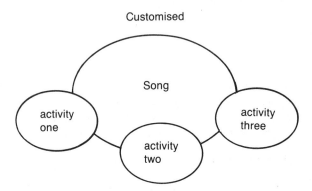

A third possibility is to consider the song in relation to your class and your pedagogical aim and choose activities on that basis. For example, some classes might not need as much work with vocabulary and activities that focus on vocabulary could be omitted as you move directly to discussion.

Getting Started

Following are groups of activities that can be used as lesson plans. They are numbered and listed with a song type they work best with. For a more complete description of the song type, see What are song types? on pages 11−12.

Short and slow songs

Lesson plan 1

Introduce the short and slow song with **Drawing the song (2)** and/or **Pictures (3)**. Give students the lyrics with **The cloze passage (23)**. Then **Song cards (20)** for a game. If you want to sing, look at **Singing with a little help from my friends (41)**. If discussion is desired, try **Picture selection (55)**.

Lesson plan 2

This is another lesson plan for short and slow songs. Begin with **All-purpose questions (24)** (count the number of times you hear . . .). Then try **Strip songs (16)** and **Lists (35)**. Many times you can sing short and slow songs. Try **Human tape recorder (42)**. Finish with **Song posters (48)**.

A selection of short and slow songs

Following is a selection of short and slow songs, listed by performer with album name and number.

Julie Andrews: *Edelweiss* (*The Sound of Music*, RCA RCP-1558).
The Beach Boys: *White Christmas* (*The Beach Boys' Christmas Album*, Capitol Records 4MX-2-164).
Tony Bennett: *I Left My Heart in San Francisco* (*Tony Bennett: San Francisco*, DTO 10040A).
Billie Holiday: *Solitude* (*The Billie Holiday Story*, MCA C2-4006).
Kiri Te Kanawa: *Blue Skies* (*Kiri Blue Skies*, London 414 666-4).

Bette Midler: *The Rose* (*The Rose*, Atlantic CS 16010).
Willie Nelson: *Georgia on My Mind* (*Stardust*, Columbia FCT 35305).
The Platters: *Summertime* (*The Great Pretender*, TIG 61).
Linda Ronstadt: *My Funny Valentine* (*For Sentimental Reasons*, Elektra/Asylum 9-60474-4-E).
James Taylor: *Isn't It Nice to be Home Again* (*Mud Slide Slim and the Blue Horizon*, Warner Bros M5 2561).

Songs that tell stories

Lesson plan 1

Introduce the song with **Tell them a story (17)**. Then use **Breathing easy (36)** to give the lyrics. Use **Song word puzzles (11)** for further vocabulary consolidation and finally **Dialogue drama (47)** to create simple dialogues based on the song lyrics.

Lesson plan 2

Another group of techniques that works well with story songs is **Rods to tell the story (4)** to introduce the story by giving students the basic story plot, **Strip songs (16)** to give the lyrics, **Paraphrasing (43)** to work with meaning, concluding with **Guided story writing (46)** or discussion with **Point of view (59)**.

A selection of songs that tell stories

Following is a selection of songs that tell stories, listed by performer with album name and number.

American Traditional: *Frankie and Johnny* (*Songs Alive*, BBC English).
Ruben Blades: *The Hit* (*Nothing but the Truth*, Elektra 9-60754-4).
Johnny Cash: *A Boy Named Sue* (*This is Johnny Cash*, CBK 3014).
Harry Chapin: *Cat's in the Cradle* (*Even if You Can't Carry a Tune*, New York: Regents Publishing Inc.).
Harry Chapin: *Taxi* (*Harry Chapin Greatest Stories Live*, Elektra C2-6003).
Barry Manilow: *Copacabana* (*Barry Manilow Greatest Hits*, Max 1561).
Shangri-Las: *Leader of the Pack* (*Original Rock & Roll*, GT 5-6251).
Bruce Springsteen: *Darlington County* (*Born in the USA*, QCT 38653).
Kenny Rogers: *The Gambler* (*Kenny Rogers Greatest Hits*, 4LV-51152).

Instrumental music

This is any music without words. A single activity will probably work better than two or three combined activities. Try **Visualisation (53), Song strings (54)** or **Multiple choice (60)**.

Long songs

Long songs are songs longer than three or three and a half minutes. This is a very large group of songs, probably the majority of published songs. For that reason there is no sample listing. Most long songs are fast but a few are slow, e.g. Billy Joel's *I'm in a New York State of Mind*. Because of their diversity this group is difficult to suggest lesson plans for.

Lesson plan 1

For a lower-level class, begin with **All-purpose questions (24)** (before listening questions section).

Then **Vocabulary songs (7)**. Continue with **Mistakes (12)** and conclude a vocabulary activity with easy discussion, **Vocabulary association (9)**.

Lesson plan 2

For an intermediate class introduce the song with **Breathing easy (36)**. Then work with the meaning using **Clichés, proverbs and sayings (63)**, or **Theme words (66)**.

Lesson plan 3

Another group of techniques is **Structure review (21)** to introduce the song. Then work with vocabulary with **Word swatter (18)**. For a discussion of the song theme use **Grammar letter (51)** or **Values (65)**.

Lesson plan 4

Some songs are very fast with almost impossible to catch lyrics, yet have interesting themes and vocabulary. Introduce this type of song with **Pop songs (32)** and continue with **Discussion questions (57)** or any of the activities above.

Short and fast songs

Lesson plan 1

Begin with **Vocabulary songs (7)** or **Vocabulary competition (13)**. Continue with **Word swatter (18)** or **Headlines (19)**. For a lower-level class stop at this point. For an intermediate class continue with a discussion activity such as **Values (65)**.

Lesson plan 2

Introduce the song with **Did you hear it? (30)**. Hand out the lyrics using **Vocabulary songs (7)**. Continue with **Definitions (14)** although **Song word puzzles (11)** and **Mistakes (12)** will work with almost any song. Conclude with **Lists (35)** for an easy discussion or **Theme words (66)** for an intermediate class.

A selection of short and fast songs

Following is a selection of short and fast songs, listed by performer with album name and number.

Julie Andrews: *My Favourite Things* (*Sound of Music*, RCA RCP-1558).
Bing Crosby: *God Rest Ye Merry Gentlemen* (MCA VCM-1501).
Ella Fitzgerald: *I Get a Kick out of You* (*Dream Dancing*, Pablo MTF 1097).
Waylon Jennings: *A Legend in My Time* (*The Taker/Tulsa*, RCA PK-1695).
Carl Perkins: *Blue Suede Shoes* (*Original Rock & Roll*, GT5-6251).
Linda Ronstadt: *Am I Blue* (*For Sentimental Reasons*, Elektra 6047-4-E).
Bruce Springsteen: *I'm on Fire* (*Born in the USA*, CBS QCT 38653).
Hank Williams Jr: *My Girl Don't Like My Cowboy Hat* (*Montana Cafe*, WB 25412-4).

INDEXES

Index of activities

The number preceding each activity is the activity number; following each activity is the page number.

Skill index

This index lists song and music activities not listed under the five main categories: vocabulary extension, listening development, singing, writing development and discussion. For example, the activity Drawing the song (2) is listed as the first activity under Vocabulary Extension. Here it is cross-referenced under 'Drawing'.

Drawing

Drawing the song (2)
Guided story writing (46)
Visualisation (53)
Picture selection (55)
Theme words (66)

Instrumental music

BGM (25)
Movies in your mind (50)
Theme music (52)
Visualisation (53)
Song strings (54)
Picture selection (Extension 2) (55)
Multiple choice (60)
Sounds nice (72)
Sound quiz (74)

Listening skills

Vocabulary prediction (1)
Drawing the song (2)
Pictures (3)
Rods to tell the story (4)
Rhyme after rhyme (5)
Vocabulary songs (7)
Alphabetical vocabulary (8)
Vocabulary association (9)
Mistakes (12)
Vocabulary competition (13)
Dictation (44)
Punctuation (49)
Grammar letter (51)
Picture selection (55)
Multiple choice (60)
Where is the music? (61)
Theme words (66)

No songs or music required for these discussion techniques

Where is the music? (61)
Musical memories (62)
Musical survey (64)
Tell me a song about . . . (67)
Jacket covers (70)
Trivia (71)
Sounds nice (72)
Songs that say a lot (73)
Sound quiz (74)

Paraphrasing

Tell them a story (17)
Paraphrasing (43)

Singing

Song cards (20)
Dictation (44)
More dictation (45)

Story telling

Rods to tell the story (4)
Strip songs (16)
Tell them a story (17)
Paraphrasing (43)
Guided story writing (46)
Dialogue drama (47)
Grammar letter (51)
Split songs (56)
Point of view (59)

Structural-grammatical

Drawing the song (2)
Rhyme after rhyme (5)
Mistakes (12)
Structural review (21)
The cloze passage (23)
All-purpose questions (24)
Lists (35)
Breathing easy (36)
Grammar letter (51)
Theme music (52)
Song strings (54)
Trivia (71)

Vocabulary

Word swatter (18)
Making connections (29)
Did you hear it? (30)
Scrambled lyrics (37)
More dictation (45)
Clichés, proverbs and sayings (63)
Theme words (66)
Abstract words (69)
Cultural stereotypes (75)

Writing

Rhyme after rhyme (5)
Vocabulary association (9)
Vocabulary competition (13)
Tell them a story (17)
Structure review (21)
Jumbled words (22)
The cloze passage (23)
BGM (Creative Writing) (25)
Titles (31)
Lists (35)

Index of activities by learner level

All the activities in this book are graded according to three levels: very low, low and intermediate. In particular they are put in a range between two of the levels. Thus the exercise Lists (35) is appropriate for students in the range of very low to intermediate. In this index the song activities will be grouped under three headings: very low and low; very low to intermediate; and intermediate. Admittedly these are relative terms, but they have some value for classroom teachers. It is frequently the case that an activity which is listed very low or low can also be used for an intermediate class, but the reverse is not always the case. The distinguishing feature of the intermediate level is that it presupposes that students can engage in discussion.

Very low to low

Alphabetical vocabulary (8)
Structure review (21)
Jumbled words (22)
Making connections (29)

Low to intermediate

Vocabulary prediction (1)
Drawing the song (2)
Pictures (3)
Rods to tell the story (4)
Rhyme after rhyme (5)
Scrambled words (6)
Vocabulary songs (7)
Take it or leave it (10)
Song word puzzles (11)
Mistakes (12)
Vocabulary competition (13)
Definitions (14)
Song poetry (15)
Strip songs (16)
Tell them a story (17)
Word swatter (18)
Headlines (19)
Song cards (20)
The cloze passage (23)

All-purpose questions (24)
BGM (25)
The top twenty (26)
Title matchings (27)
Review quiz (28)
Did you hear it? (30)
Pop songs (32)
Rhythm and stress (33)
Two versions (34)
Lists (35)
Breathing easy (36)
Scrambled lyrics (37)
Song corner (38)
Strike up the band (39)
Mini musicals (40)
Singing with a little help from
  my friends (41)
Human tape recorder (42)
Dictation (44)
More dictation (45)
Guided story writing (46)
Dialogue drama (47)
Song posters (48)
Punctuation (49)
Grammar letter (51)
Theme music (52)
Song strings (54)
Picture selection (55)
Discussion questions (57)

Where is the music? (61)
Music survey (64)
Theme words (66)
Tell me a song about . . . (67)
Song competition (68)
Abstract words (69)
Sounds nice (72)
Songs that say a lot (73)
Sound quiz (74)
Cultural stereotypes (75)

Intermediate

Vocabulary association (9)
Titles (31)
Paraphrasing (43)
Movies in your mind (50)
Visualisation (53)
Split songs (56)
Feelings (58)
Point of view (59)
Multiple choice (60)
Musical memories (62)
Clichés, proverbs and sayings
  (63)
Values (65)
Jacket covers (70)
Trivia (71)
Video warm up (76)

Index of songs mentioned in activities

Following are the popular songs cited as examples in the activities. Some well-known classical music selections are not included.

Performer, song title, album   Activities

Performer, song title, album	Activities
Patti Austin: *True Love* (*The Real Me*, Quest Warner Bros 4-25696).	51
Tony Bennet: *I Left My Heart in San Francisco* (*San Francisco*, DTO 10040A).	2
Chuck Berry: *Reelin' and Rockin'* (*The Best of the Best of Chuck Berry*, GT-5-0004).	35
Johnny Cash: *Easy Street* (*Rainbow*, CBS FCT 39951).	68
Johnny Cash: *Big River* (*Johnny Cash, Greatest Hits*, CBS 25AP 2256).	35
Chinese Classical Music (Fung Hang Records CCMC 09).	54
Echo and the Bunnymen: *Blue Blue Ocean* (Sire Records, WB 25597-4).	15
Benny Goodman: *Let's Dance* (Capitol 4XL-9090).	54
Joni James: *These Foolish Things* (*Joni James 20 Greatest Hits*, NC 833320).	35
Cyndi Lauper: *Money Changes Everything* (*She's So Unusual*, Portrait FRT 38930).	68
Polly Merdinger and Joel Rosenfeld 1884: *The Marvellous Toy* eds, *Even If You Can't Carry a Tune* (Newbury House, Rowley, Mass.).	2
Willie Nelson: *September Song* (*Stardust*, CBS FCT 35305).	68
Willie Nelson: *Moonlight in Vermont* (*Stardust*, CCS FCT 35305).	35
Platters: *September Song* (*The Great Pretender*, TIG 61).	68
Pointer Sisters: *Santa Claus is Coming to Town* (*A Very Special Christmas*).	51
Jean-Pierre Rampal: *Japanese Folk Melodies* (CBS MT 35862).	68
Lou Reed: *September Song* (*Lost in the Stars: The music of Kurt Weill*, AMC-28083).	68
Ravi Shankar: *The Genius of Ravi Shankar* (CBS PCT 9560).	54
Paul Simon: *When Numbers Get Serious* (*Hearts and Bones*, WB 92-3942-4).	35
Paul Simon: *Homeless* (*Graceland*, Warner Bros PKG-3177).	15
Bruce Springsteen: *Bobby Jean* (*Born in the USA*, CBS QCT 38653).	57
James Taylor: *Isn't It Nice to be Home Again* (*Mud Slide Slim and the Blue Horizon*, WB M5 256).	66
Kiri Te Kanawa: *True Love* (*Kiri, Blue Skies*, London 414 666-4).	51